KNIGHTS
OF THE
MEDIEVAL WORLD

FROM HOUSEHOLD GUARD TO COURTLY LOVER

PHYLLIS JESTICE

Published by
Amber Books Ltd
United House
North Road
London
N7 9DP
United Kingdom
www.amberbooks.co.uk
Appstore: itunes.com/apps/amberbooksltd
Facebook: www.facebook.com/amberbooks
Twitter: @amberbooks

ISBN: 978-1-78274-731-4

Project Editor: Michael Spilling
Designer: Zoe Mellors
Picture Research: Terry Forshaw

Printed in Italy

KNIGHTS
OF THE
MEDIEVAL
WORLD

Contents

ous tristan qui li durement le
roit de la duentine de dinadan q
a pou quil neuiuoit deus pour
œ quil sauoit bien dut le seau
ne estoit vain ne il ne vuelt m
que mul autre le pzrte dist alez
aner traine de lauuine pour
uanime pzandze autte ta

Origins

Knighthood and chivalry formed an essential part of society in the European Middle Ages, even more important in the popular imagination than they were in reality. Medieval people themselves believed there had been knights – and the value system associated with knights known as 'chivalry' – for nearly all of human history.

As the social commentator Ramon Lull reports in his late-thirteenth-century *Book of the Order of Chivalry*, after Adam and Eve were expelled from Paradise, wars soon broke out, a natural consequence of Original Sin. The world was rapidly descending into chaos: in order to 'defend and restrain' the people, it was necessary, Lull says, to invent chivalry. Rulers selected one out of each thousand men – the strongest, noblest and most loyal available – equipping them as knights, and there have been knights ever since.

Lull's account neatly sums up medieval beliefs of what knights were, or ought to be. They were the military experts of the Middle Ages: professionals who fought in heavy armour from horseback. But they were much more than brutal fighting machines. To be a good knight, one should also fight for worthy causes, loyally supporting one's lord and comrades, and displaying all the personal characteristics that the age defined as 'noble'. Needless to say, not all knights lived up to Lull's ideal vision, but the lives of all knights were at least in part shaped by the cultural expectations that Lull takes for granted.

Medieval audiences assumed that European cavalry forces throughout history fought and behaved as their contemporaries did. Thus, all men of the past who had fought on horseback were knights, and Europeans assumed that cavalrymen of all ages embodied the ethical system considered ideal among their contemporaries.

Facing page: In this thirteenth-century French illustration, the king strikes a perfect jousting blow, hitting his opponent on the visor of the helmet.

Right: Alexander the Great, famed for taming the horse Bucephalus, was the world's first famous cavalry commander.

Above: The Jewish hero Judas Maccabeus probably fought on foot, but medieval legend transformed him into a knight, one of the Nine Worthies.

Such a belief is summed up in medieval tales of the 'Nine Worthies' – the greatest knights of all time. The list includes such figures as Alexander the Great and Judas Maccabeus, who in art are depicted as medieval knights, because that is the way audiences thought of them. This belief in the age-old nature of knighthood makes it difficult for modern scholars to figure out when in fact knighthood developed.

In reality, what we think of as a 'knight' – a heavily armoured man for whom warfare was his main profession, who typically fought on horseback and who was constrained by a distinct code of ethical behaviour – gradually evolved in the central Middle Ages. It is only in the twelfth century that we can see fighting men who would be fully recognizable to the popular imagination as medieval knights. A number of elements had to come together to create knights, knighthood and chivalry.

FROM HOUSEHOLD BANDS TO ELITE CAVALRY FORCE

The earliest element that went into the creation of the knight was the professional fighting man. Kings and great lords from the dawn of the Middle Ages maintained some household troops – men who ordinarily served as the core of military levies. These household retainers were usually professional fighters; they had no other regular occupation such as farming. They would have originated from a range of social classes, including the younger sons of nobles, but were also lower-class men who were taken from their labour in the fields and trained.

Such men, who lived and trained together, occupying their time with sport and military exercises, were recognized as a military elite. They had an edge in battle because they could fight as a team, besides enjoying the

Above: A page from the Anglo-Saxon epic poem *Beowulf* written on vellum. In his final struggle with a dragon, Beowulf's household troops abandoned him in fear, inspiring the poet to condemn battlefield disloyalty.

individual prowess of men who trained in arms year-round. But they had another real advantage besides training: far better arms and armour than the average man who was only called up occasionally for military service. One can see as early as texts such as *Beowulf* (which probably reached its final form by c. 800) that war bands were well equipped: the poet speaks of the fine hauberks and helmets of Beowulf's followers, not to mention their precious swords.

The lord would have provided this equipment, making his men more formidable in battle and displaying his own wealth in this way. This was gear beyond the reach of even a prosperous farmer, who would have gone to war wearing leather and carrying a wooden shield, bearing as offensive weapons the much cheaper spear or axe instead of the elite sword.

Thus, already in the early medieval war band, we can see two important elements of the future knight: professionalism and good equipment. Indeed, good equipment later in the Middle Ages was an essential hallmark of knights. It is frequently argued that knights' heavy armour, developed from the gear of household troops, was the most essential feature of knightly warfare, since a knight's armour played a decisive role in battles whether he was mounted or on foot.

Whether he fought from horseback or not, the knight of the

Right: Only Lancelot's love for Queen Guinevere made it possible for him to bear the shame of riding in a cart after his steed was killed by enemies.

high Middle Ages was by definition a horseman. He received golden spurs upon entry into knighthood and, as we will see, would be dishonoured if he travelled by any means except horse. Indeed, in the twelfth-century romance that first introduced Sir Lancelot to the medieval world, the plot revolves around the fact that, while Lancelot was riding to save Queen Guinevere from an enemy, his horse was killed. To continue on his quest, he was forced to accept a ride in a cart – his great sacrifice in allowing himself to be dishonoured by doing so being proof of his love for the queen.

THE DEVELOPMENT OF CAVALRY FORCES

Cavalry only gradually came to occupy an essential place in medieval armies, a position it attained probably in the ninth century. Nobles had always ridden as a mark of their rank, but, like the Anglo-Saxons up until the time of the Norman Conquest, their usual practice was to dismount to fight. Still, any Germanic war band would have included some horsemen, as they were invaluable for scouting, quick raids, or pursuing a fleeing enemy. Except among the Franks, though, early medieval war bands normally fought on foot. As in many other elements of medieval society, the Franks were innovators, probably spurred on by the need to combat Muslim raiders who crossed the Pyrenees from Spain. By the eighth century, the Carolingian rulers of the Kingdom of the Franks had seen the usefulness of cavalry: well-handled cavalry could play a vital role in breaking up the enemies' infantry formations, was capable of rendering victories decisive by pursuing fleeing foes, and provided mobility for

ET SYRIAM SOBAL · ET CONVERTIT

raids. Charlemagne (768–814) in particular gave cavalry a new prominence, ordering that all significant landowners own a full coat of armour and weapons and serve as cavalry upon demand. At least ten per cent of his army consisted of cavalry.

Cavalry became yet more central to the military forces of both halves of the Frankish Empire in the course of the tenth century. Charlemagne's empire divided into western (France) and eastern (Germany) parts after 840, and both kingdoms warred frequently with internal rebels, external invaders, and each other. Especially in France, the central authority of the state largely disintegrated,

Above: Ninth-century Frankish cavalry. Note that they use stirrups, but carry simple spears rather than heavier lances.

putting a premium on nobles' well-trained fighting forces. Frequent Viking raids also taught how important it was to be able to move troops at faster than walking pace,

The Importance Of The Stirrup

There is much dispute over the role of the stirrup in the development of this Frankish cavalry force. The original argument was that, without stirrups to anchor the rider securely in the saddle, it is impossible to strike heavy blows without falling off. Therefore, the historian Lynn White argued that the introduction of the stirrup was revolutionary in Europe: because the Franks adopted it first, they won a decisive edge in battle that allowed them not only to defeat the Muslims but also to win a great empire. Historians today agree that the Carolingians gave cavalry more and more prominence over time. We also know that Carolingian cavalrymen used stirrups, but the evidence has shown that the introduction of stirrups was not a

Left: A simple saddle and stirrup, as would have been used by cavalrymen in the ninth and tenth centuries.

sudden innovation. Instead, they were only gradually adopted over several centuries.

Moreover, studies have shown that a high, supportive saddle, such as was already used in Roman times, provides nearly as much security on horseback as stirrups. Therefore, it is no longer possible to regard stirrups as a transformative technology. It seems more likely that cavalry forces came into being when rulers and lords had the resources to equip and train them to fight effectively. Cavalrymen then gradually adopted tools (like stirrups) that made their job easier. It is hard to piece together the history of cavalry fighting from the fragmentary sources of the ninth century, but scholars agree that cavalry played an increasingly prominent role in Carolingian armies.

"…the greatest catalyst to creating a full cavalry force was the Magyars, mounted raiders from the east."

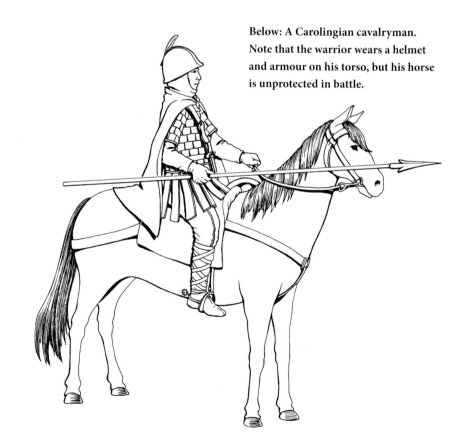

Below: A Carolingian cavalryman. Note that the warrior wears a helmet and armour on his torso, but his horse is unprotected in battle.

as Viking bands usually obtained horses as quickly as possible. By about 1000, the importance of the French 'royal cavalry' is clear in the work of the historian Richer, but it is hard to see details of their evolution or function.

GAINING POWER THROUGH CAVALRY

The move of heavily armed cavalry to centre stage is clearer in the case of Germany, where a new dynasty, the Ottonians, came to power in 919. The Ottonians, before becoming kings, were dukes of the Saxons, who had traditionally fought on foot. The influx of a new Frankish ruling class with the Carolingian conquest of Saxony at the end of the eighth century would have created a greater awareness of the advantages of cavalry fighting. However, the greatest catalyst to creating a full

cavalry force was the Magyars, mounted raiders from the east. Like the steppe peoples in general, they fought from horseback with compound bows and spears. Unlike the usual Viking raid, Magyar raiding bands numbered in the thousands, devastating large swathes of territory. Only a large and well-organized army could hope to survive confrontation with the Magyars.

The first encounters of German armies with the Magyars in the late ninth century showed the ineffectiveness of German military organization against this new threat. A mostly infantry army lacked the mobility to succeed against a foe that specialized in hit-and-run tactics, circling and shooting arrows at their less mobile foe or drawing the Germans out in feigned retreats, only to turn on them. In 907, the Magyars

destroyed a Bavarian army; then the following year defeated and killed the Duke of Thuringia in another bloody battle. In 910, the invaders soundly defeated a united German army near Augsburg, inducing the Germans to abandon their shield wall by feigning retreat, then wheeling to attack the disorganized infantrymen. For the rest of the decade, Magyar raiders were able to loot almost at will in the German kingdom, reaching as far as modern Switzerland and northern Italy.

The situation was reversed when the dynamic Henry I of Saxony was elected king of the Germans in 919. He made a truce with the Magyars (paying

Below: A romanticised view of Magyars, whose raids devastated much of Europe until they were decisively defeated by the Ottonian rulers of Germany.

> *"A massed charge of the German heavy cavalry proved devastating against the mounted but poorly armed Magyars."*

them tribute) and employed the breathing space he gained in this way to improve the training and equipment of a heavy cavalry force. The sources describe these fighting men as *loricati* – men wearing heavy armour – but it is clear from the chronicles that they fought on horseback with spears and swords. These *loricati* were recruited from among the nobles of Germany, although, as in earlier times, the king or a great lord would have provided equipment for members of his military household.

The German cavalry force first proved its effectiveness in the Battle of Lenzen against the Slavic Redarii in 929. During this, a well-timed cavalry charge routed the Slavic force and then slaughtered the foes as they fled.

Emboldened by his success, Henry I then refused to pay tribute to the Magyars in 932. When the Magyars responded with a major raid into Germany, Henry met them with an army that included cavalry levied from every region of his kingdom. A massed charge of the German heavy cavalry proved devastating against the mounted but poorly armed Magyar riders.

THE LAST OF THE MAGYARS

By the time of the last major German battle with the Magyars, the Battle of Lechfeld in 955, Henry's son, Otto I of Germany, probably had between 3000 and 4000 cavalry at his command. By this time, the German cavalry forces were disciplined and their leaders had enough experience to use them effectively. The Magyars tried to draw their enemies out of their tight formations with a feigned retreat, but the Germans refused to take the bait. Even when the Magyars broke off the fight

and began to withdraw, Otto's forces maintained their discipline, methodically pursuing and killing many of the invaders.

The result was a German victory so decisive that it ended the era of Magyar raids to the west. It was the combination of horses and heavy armour at Otto's command that proved so effective. The German army would have been unable to engage with the mounted Magyars if they themselves had not been able to deploy a large cavalry force. But in the one-on-one fighting that ensued, the German *loricati* had a decisive advantage, since most of the Magyars did not wear body armour. Armour – expensive hauberks and helmets in particular – was simply out of the reach of most people in the

borderlands. Indeed, in 990, a Slavic prince was advised not to try to fight the Saxons who were invading his lands. Although they only had a small force, he was told, they were all excellent warriors, and were all in iron.

THE EXPENSE OF MAINTAINING CAVALRY

Even in the more settled lands, finding the money to equip heavy cavalry was a great challenge. As we will see in Chapter 3, a hauberk of iron rings was enormously expensive, both because of the hundreds of hours of work involved in making it and because of the high cost of the iron itself. Similarly, a good sword was a masterpiece of artisanship and very expensive. At least the armour was

Above: The Battle of Lechfeld was such a major victory that Otto I won the title "the Great" and was soon acclaimed as emperor.

relatively durable, but a cavalryman needed several horses as well, and the attrition of horses in a hard-fought campaign would have been staggering. An important question for any lord of the tenth century must have been whether he could get enough use out of heavy cavalry to justify the great cost. There were two compelling reasons to invest in cavalry, however: if your king or other overlord made you do so, or if the neighbours had equipped cavalry and were liable to attack you if you didn't protect yourself. Some regions, such as England, made next to no use of cavalry in this period, because the Welsh, Scots, and Vikings whom they combatted did not use horses in battle.

In France and Germany, a domino effect was well under way by the time Otto I fought at Lechfeld. Since the Saxons had heavy cavalry, the Bavarians had to follow suit, while to the west, French royal forces had to keep up with their own acquisitive and power-hungry nobles as well as the strong German state. The key unit of this new heavy cavalry remained the military household, with individual nobles responsible for equipping their own fighting men.

We can see this system in a unique document from 981, the *Indiculus loricatorum*, created when German Emperor Otto II summoned an additional 2000 heavy cavalry from home to support

Below: An excerpt from the Indiculus loricatorum of 981, laying out how many heavy cavalrymen a number of monasteries should provide for Otto II's army.

Above: This illustration from the thirteenth-century *Sachsenspiegel* (Mirror of Saxons) shows a knight receiving payment from one of his serfs.

his campaign against the Muslims in southern Italy. The summons was issued to the great landowners, each of whom had to provide a fixed quota of men, all equipped with the proper arms and armour. It is clear that many of these men came from the lower class, and owed their equipment to their lord. In fact, many of these fighting men would have been serfs, legally unfree and dependent on their lord.

Germany was wealthy in the tenth century, and a considerable number of great lords (whether dukes, counts, bishops or abbots)

could afford to equip and maintain elite household troops year-round: men who ate at their table and slept in their halls. Such a system had serious disadvantages, however. While a lord would always have kept at least some retainers on hand, it was very expensive to provide an entire large war band with food and drink all year, even though there was normally only fighting in the summer.

In the cash-poor society of the tenth century, paying the fighting men, especially buying their equipment and horses, could put an intolerable strain on resources. Lords derived most of their income from the rents owed by their agricultural labourers, who in turn required supervision. Increasingly, the great lords turned to a simple solution. Instead of paying stewards to manage estates, providing the money needed to equip heavy cavalrymen, why not just put the estates under the direct authority of the fighters? Fighters could live on the estate that had

> *"Germany was wealthy in the tenth century, and a considerable number of great lords… could afford to equip and maintain elite household troops year-round…"*

been placed in their charge most of the year and could supply their own equipment from the revenues

Below: This reenactor is wearing a Viking-style helmet and hauberk, but has added a chain mail veil and gloves. Equipment of early knights would have varied greatly depending on personal taste.

generated. Thus the *fief* was born: a conditional grant of land in return for military service. Although only a minority of knights were fortunate enough to become fief-holders, control of land and the peasants who worked it helped to raise the social class of heavy cavalrymen.

FROM FIGHTING MAN TO GENTLEMAN

By the beginning of the eleventh century, recognizable bodies of professional mounted fighting men who were protected with iron hauberks and helmets existed in most of the core lands of Europe. It would be a mistake to think of them as a social 'class' in this period, though. Rather, there existed at least two clearly distinguishable groups among the ranks of the heavy cavalrymen. On the one hand were the nobles. Nobles were expected to lead their household troops in battle. When equipped, they probably looked much like the men under their command, except for the finer workmanship of hauberk

Right: A modern painting showing the Norman charge at Hastings. The man with the club is Bishop Odo of Bayeux; as a priest, he could not shed human blood.

"The noble and his sons were part of the ruling elite, with an assured place at court, displaying manners appropriate to their elite status and often even literate."

and sword, perhaps even with decoration applied to helmets and shields.

However, a lord in the tenth century would never have described himself as a *miles* – a mounted heavy cavalryman. The noble and his sons were part of the ruling elite, with an assured place at court, displaying manners appropriate to their elite status and often even literate. They were very different from the lord's poor dependants, unlettered and uncultured, equipped as heavy cavalry only thanks to the arbitrary choice of their lord. The social status of these *milites* was uncertain, but was certainly different from that of their lords. Were members of this larger, mostly nameless, mass of fighting men 'knights'? They were according to the original meaning

of the word. Our word 'knight' comes from the Anglo-Saxon, and was used to describe the heavy cavalry who came to England in 1066 with William the Conqueror. The original form, *cniht*, means 'servant'. This word origin is a useful reminder that as late as 1066

most French knights were a far cry from the nobility we associate with knighthood today.

Many knightly families may have begun with an ancestor who was a serf, chosen for military service because of strong muscles and a steady eye. Still, even if such

a man was legally unfree, he was privileged, as were the Mamluks of medieval Egypt or the Janissaries of the Ottoman Empire. After all, it hardly pays to treat the members of an armed fighting elite poorly. The German lands continued to have a large number of 'serf-knights'

"A mounted warrior given a grant of land… had resources at his command. As a result, his social status began to rise significantly…"

(*ministeriales*) until the end of the twelfth century. These men were often granted fiefs, but remained legally unfree and therefore subject to their lord's will. The existence of the German *ministeriales* created particular tensions in German society, because the members of that class were eager to embrace the values and privileges coming to be identified with the rank of 'knight'. As early as 1127, northern European society was shocked when the members of a *ministerial* family banded together to murder their lord, Count Charles the Good of Flanders. They had passed for free knights, but the count had discovered their true, unfree status and threatened them with an unbearable loss of status.

ARISING THROUGH THE RANKS

By 1127, when Charles the Good lay dead in the church of St Donatian, Bruges, to be a knight was clearly to be the free member of a social elite. The reason for this elevation in rank lies with the resources that were increasingly entrusted to knights. A mounted warrior given a grant of land to support and provide for himself had resources at his command. As a result, his social status began to rise significantly in the eleventh century. A fief-holder could provide for a wife and children, himself equipping his sons to fight as heavy cavalrymen. And he would certainly identify himself as something different from the

peasants who worked his estate. These fighting men began imitating the lifestyle of the nobility, aspiring to purchase expensive imported goods or demonstrating how cultured they were by patronizing poets and musicians.

The way to gain that essential fief was through military prowess. A daring, well-armed equestrian who could prove his loyalty and find a place for himself in a royal court could dream large dreams. Two examples demonstrate how the world opened up for the first recognizable knights of the eleventh century.

Rodrigo Díaz de Vivar (1043–99) was a Castilian, the son of a minor knightly family. He was raised at the royal court, and his fighting skill led to great honours, including service as the king's standard-bearer and important military commands. As a result of court intrigue, Rodrigo was exiled, but had such a formidable military reputation that he soon found service with the Muslim emir of Zaragoza. In time, Rodrigo conquered Valencia for himself,

ruling it as prince until his death. He became known by his Arabic nickname – El Cid ('the Lord') – and is still remembered as a national hero of Spain.

Another son of a minor knight, Robert Guiscard, was the Cid's exact contemporary. Robert 'the Wily' was a Norman, the sixth son of a large family whose parents could barely afford to equip their sons with arms and send them into the world to seek their fortune. Along with most of his brothers, Robert made his way to southern Italy, where the Lombards were hiring mercenaries to help in their constant wars against Muslims, Byzantines, and each other. Through a combination of ruthlessness and luck, Robert first became leader of a large band of Norman knights in Italy, then successfully made himself Duke of Apulia. His was one of the great success stories of the eleventh century, and his descendants became kings of Sicily.

Many poor knights must have encouraged themselves with tales

Above: Jan van Beers' early twentieth-century painting of the funeral of Charles the Good of Flanders catches much of the shock contemporaries felt at his assassination by his own vassals.

Below: El Cid, commemorated with his faithful steed Babieca with a statue in Burgos, Spain. When his master died, Babieca refused to ever allow another man to mount him.

> *"The shock of a single knight and his horse charging in this way would have been overwhelming, able to break through an enemy line much like a modern tank."*

of such rewards for the brave and fortunate. One should of course remember that, for every named Norman adventurer in the conquest of southern Italy and eventually Sicily, there were hundreds of other knights whose exploits never made it into the annals. And, for all the impressiveness of an eleventh-century knight, clad in iron and mounted on a well-trained warhorse, it was knights working together as a team who made a decisive difference on battlefields.

THE ADVANTAGE OF THE LANCE

It takes very well disciplined infantry to stand steady against the terror of a massed cavalry charge. It *could* be resisted, as the Anglo-Saxons showed at the Battle of Hastings in 1066. In that case, well-armed and disciplined household troops formed a dense shield wall, against which the Norman knights of William the Conqueror charged in vain. It was only after the ranks of the shield wall had been thinned

Facing page: In this nineteenth-century engraving, Robert Guiscard launches the Norman invasion of Sicily, which in fact was largely carried out by his brother Roger Borsa.

by repeated archery onslaughts (King Harold Godwinson fell, an arrow in his eye), and the Anglo-Saxon warriors voluntarily broke formation to chase after apparently defeated knights who were only pretending to flee that William won the day. At Hastings, most of the Norman cavalrymen fought with swords or with spears used in the traditional way, to judge from the evidence of the Bayeux Tapestry. In other words, they jabbed with their relatively thin spears, either overhand or underhand, as the horses milled along the edge of the shield wall and the Normans tried to find a means to break through.

However, a new, distinctive fighting method was developing in the second half of the eleventh century, and perhaps had already been employed in the Normans' wars of conquest in southern Italy. This was a cavalry charge employing a heavier spear – a lance – that was now wedged tightly under the knight's arm and held parallel with the ground. By holding the lance in this 'couched' position, the knight could focus his whole body weight, as well as that of his horse, behind the point of the lance.

The first literary work to describe a cavalry engagement taking place with couched lances is the *Song of Roland*, written in c. 1100. The author does not treat it as a novelty, so it is likely the technique had been around for. at least a generation. The shock of a single knight and his horse charging in this way would have been overwhelming, able to break through an enemy line much like a modern tank.

The Byzantine historian Anna Comnena, who observed Norman knights both in their attacks on her father's empire and during the First Crusade, commented that a mounted 'Celt' (as she called the westerners) in his heavy armour would be able to bore through the walls of Babylon. Awesome as such a charge by a single knight might be, though, what made this new fighting technique truly devastating was that knights would charge in teams, working together in repeated thrusts intended to shred infantry resistance. For centuries, it was a rare force of footmen that could stand up to a charge of knights with couched lances. By the beginning of the twelfth century, rulers had come to rely on the knightly charge as the game-changer in battle.

THE TWELFTH-CENTURY KNIGHT

By the twelfth century, the knight had penetrated into at least the fringes of the nobility and began to close ranks against encroachers who tried to raise themselves to the status of knighthood. From about 1050 on, knighthood became a hereditary status, so only the

Above: The Bayeux Tapestry, 50 centimetres (20 inches) tall and nearly 70 metres (230 feet) long, tells the story of the Norman Conquest of England. This panel shows clearly the shield wall of well-armed Englishmen on the right.

son of a knight could become a knight in turn. Even in Germany, the *ministerial* serf-knights passed their fiefs and their position as a military elite on to their sons. An 1152 Germany decree even declared officially that peasants could not become knights, and further forbade either farmers or Jews from wearing a sword – demonstrating that sword bearing was a sign of knightly rank. Only in Italy did many 'new men' continue to break into the ranks of knighthood, with wealthy men equipping themselves or their sons and Italian cities

declaring the new knight's rank. The German chronicler Otto of Freising, writing in c. 1150, complained about the Italian cities' habit of making men of 'inferior status' knights, expressing in his account his own society's sense that knights occupied an elevated social status.

Only in the fourteenth century did the ranks of the knights become more exclusive in Italy as well as the rest of Europe.

By the twelfth century, a knight was 'made' at least north of the Alps – raised to a special status in a formal ceremony known as

dubbing or bestowing the accolade. Perhaps we can see an early pictorial example of this ceremony on the Bayeux Tapestry, in a panel where Duke William of Normandy (the future Conqueror) confers arms on Harold Godwinson, who had taken part in a campaign with the duke.

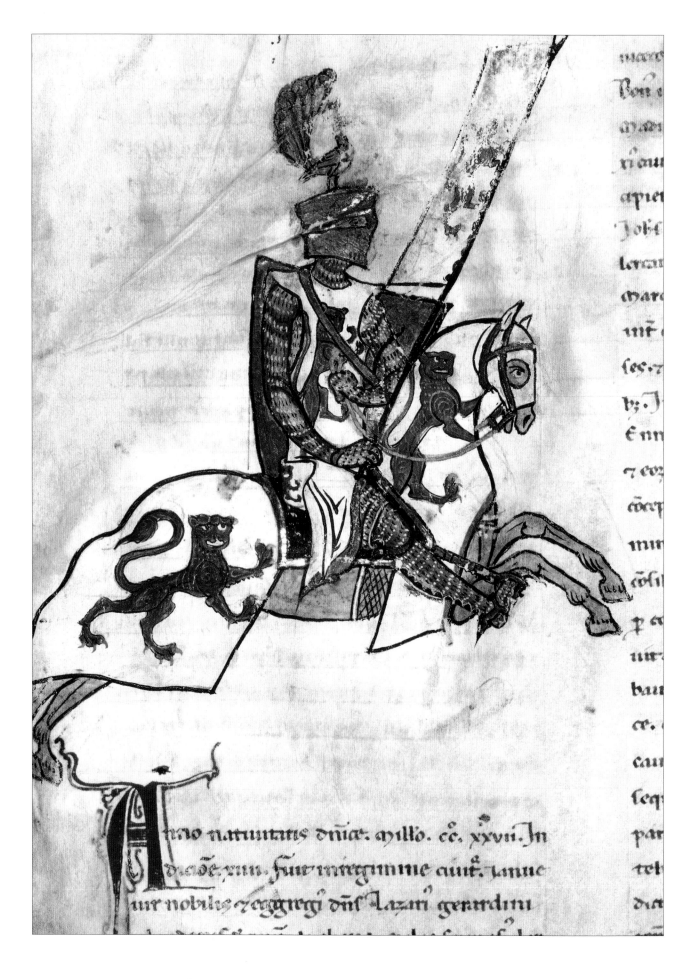

KNIGHTS AND NOBLES

It became the custom about this time for princes to be knighted to mark their passage to manhood. In fact, the German emperor Frederick Barbarossa by the 1170s was using the term *milites*, which in earlier periods had meant any professional fighting man, to describe not only members of his court but himself and his sons. The same shift occurred in England in the reign of Henry II (1154–1189). When Frederick Barbarossa knighted his two sons at Mainz in 1184, the event was a massive spectacle that attracted the awed admiration of contemporaries. It became a standard element of relations between lords and their vassals that the lord was entitled to a gift to help defray the cost when his eldest son was knighted.

It is likely that ordinary knights took pride in this recognition that they were part of the same order in society as their rulers. In the great tripartite division of society into those who work, those who fight, and those who pray, they were the fighters, the elite, the core of any military force. They clearly thought of themselves as noble. Already in about 1100, knights started using official seals, laying claim in that way to elite status.

As much as they could afford to do so, these knights modelled their behaviour on that of the higher nobility, purchasing not only expensive war steeds and armour but also luxury items like silk and spices. To do so, they exploited the peasants on the estates they controlled to the best of their ability, often forcing agricultural

The Knighthood Of Geoffrey Of Anjou

The first detailed account of making a knight is the ceremony that conferred knighthood on Geoffrey of Anjou in 1128, shortly before his marriage to King Henry I of England's daughter, Matilda. Geoffrey first underwent a ritual bath, then was dressed in a cloth of gold tunic with a purple cloak. Gold spurs were fixed on his heels and a shield hung around his neck, before the king himself girded a sword on the new knight's waist. Thirty of Geoffrey's companions were knighted at the same time, and the event was celebrated with a week of feasts and tournaments.

The surprising element in the account of Geoffrey's investiture as a knight is that we can for the first time see clearly that members of the very highest aristocracy were proud and even eager to identify themselves as knights.

Above: Geoffrey of Anjou (1113–1151), as depicted on his tomb monument. The father of Henry II of England, the heraldic device on his shield may have inspired the English royal coat of arms.

innovations to increase their incomes. Their behaviour towards their peers, too, came to imitate that of the royal and great noble courts, with the new term 'courtly' emerging late in the eleventh century to describe a standard of proper behaviour that befitted these self-styled nobles. Not every knight had a fief (England in the Norman period had about 5000 knights' fees, for example), but every knight could aspire to lordship. There were enough success stories to encourage the others.

Facing page: A knight of the mid-twelfth century. Note that he has a closed helmet, mail leggings, and a rampant lion device to identify him in battle or tournament.

"Knights received double the pay of their unknighted counterparts in most armies, despite fighting in exactly the same way with exactly the same equipment."

A famous example is that of William Marshal (1147–1219). The younger son of a knight, he was not heir to his father's fief and had few prospects besides what he could earn by his own skill. William took service with a lord and failed even to take any loot in his first military engagement, since he was so busy fighting. To make matters worse, his horse was killed, putting him in dire straits. But the young knight had impressed his superiors, who soon began rewarding William richly for his services. William won a fortune fighting in tournaments, in the process gaining an international reputation for his prowess. His fame in turn led to a special opportunity to serve as head of the military household of Henry II of England's eldest son. Finally, he won the most glowing of prizes, the hand of a great heiress, and his marriage completed his elevation from landless knight to the dazzling height of Earl of Pembroke. Few knights succeeded to such a degree as William Marshal, but lords jealously guarded their right to arrange marriages of heiresses and widows as an important means to reward faithful knights.

THE DEFENCE OF JERUSALEM

To be a knight was indeed something special. It became an honour to which sons of knightly families might aspire for years, only winning the accolade after years of faithful service on the battlefields of Europe. Knights received double the pay of their unknighted counterparts in most armies, despite fighting in exactly the same way with exactly the same equipment. Clearly, knighthood by the end of the twelfth century was thought to endow the fighting man with special qualities, including leadership skills and a sense of honour that would make a knight perform his duty to his utmost power. Only that belief can explain the events surrounding the desperate defence of Jerusalem against Saladin's onslaught in 1187.

The city's plight was practically hopeless. A large Muslim army led by the redoubtable Sultan Saladin had destroyed the army of the Kingdom of Jerusalem at the Battle of Hattin, leaving the fortresses of the Holy Land almost completely stripped of defenders. One by one, castles and towns yielded to Saladin in rapid succession. Yet the leader of Jerusalem's defence,

Facing page: Emperor Frederick I Barbarossa (1155–1190), shown here with his sons Henry and Frederick. All three were proud to be regarded as knights.

Above: This effigy of William Marshal in Temple Church, London, shows a well-equipped knight from c. 1200. The crossed legs symbolise that he went on crusade.

Baron Balian of Ibelin, had to do his best to defend that holiest of cities, not least to prevent the enslavement of the populace and the destruction of the holy places at the hands of Muslims eager to avenge the massacre of their co-religionists there in the First Crusade.

Balian decided to breathe spirit into the frightened Jerusalemites by bestowing knighthood on all noble boys in the city who were aged sixteen or older, as well as townsmen able to equip themselves for the fight. These new knights were not able to save the city, but their defence was so stout that Saladin agreed to generous terms in return for surrender, allowing most of the Christian populace to be ransomed for a nominal sum.

Could Jerusalem have been so stalwartly defended if Balian had not created new knights, willing

Above: Balian of Ibelin rallying his troops to resist Saladin's onslaught in the siege of Jerusalem, 1187.

Left: After the Battle of Hattin, the surviving Christian knights surrendered to Saladin. Note that the courteous sultan has placed the defeated King Guy beside him.

to fight to the death to defend their new honour? It is doubtful, because by that fateful year in the life of medieval Europe everyone knew that knighthood did not just mean a technique to wage combat effectively as heavy cavalry. Nor was it just an aristocratic social standing, although elevated social rank was assumed for knights by the late twelfth century. Instead, what Balian's action displays is an ethical ideal of what a knight ought to be: a set of values collectively known as 'chivalry'.

societates facte sñt quaru vna portabat Rofedaz qua
hodie dicimus rubeaz plenaz roxio albis Huius
fuit Albertus pegoletus ꝓ quod ex hñt dictꝰ est albert
Alia sonetas Iuuenu portabat ...... auxea magia i Rofed
ad ꝓtas tertam horu Iuuenu capud fuit .... de trã solgred
ex hoc .... dictꝰ est. Tꝯe vero ꝓmi federici dicti barbaxosa im
noue societates facte sunt quaru vna portauit ma ꝓilos albos i Rofeca ꜳ̃gra ꜳ̃
capud hominis nigreꝰ in campo albo cuius ꝓartis capud fuit iuliano de parad
et graso Et ꝓ hoc ipe cuꜳ̃ felis dictꝰ est de capite nigro Cuꝯ vero sem
roñdalu ortꝰ est iuter Yoñescs et patau
parte et tarcusinos ac Venctos ex alia Aj an
stefanium vicecꝯ ipialis huuisi
tates ꝓhibite fucce hñ onꝯ
t mandeciã posedit fortiñ ꝓ
quod ipe quo facta est flu
nauigatur ad motes salicꝯ
aꝯ ibi cset distructus fuit
d tuifa fuit vcla mande
partes quaru vna remã
flumes Cuiuꝯ rci fucceñ
ille de caraxia et ꝓ hoc cñ
specialiꝯ inimiciaꝯ ꝓ quã fi
multas inuecciaꝯ huic familic
Vt infra ꝓarebit Jdam enele
fuit qui asociauecat caroli
cõtra desidciū rege papie
augulo militari fuit deora
stis Vudis terum portauit ex
infra cñ de trã solgardo ꝓdicuñ
Jtem ꝓ caroli t
cun gcnuꝯ
fuit Vt di
illaciu ꝓ
ꝓalicct
ꝓariet
distraꝯ
pou
ꝓ R
vic

Chivalric Code

A new term came into use to describe knights in the late eleventh century: chivalry. In essence, the word means 'to be a knight', a fighter on horseback, since it derives from the French word for a horse (*cheval*). But already by that time to be 'chivalrous' meant more than simply wearing armour and fighting as cavalry. For contemporaries, 'chivalry' meant at the very least deeds of great valour. In the early twelfth century, the term was coming to indicate a set of ideas and practices, what a good knight ought to believe and how he ought to behave. It is the last of these meanings that is the focus of this chapter.

Many medieval authors – and many modern scholars – have struggled to define the value system of knights. There was no official 'code' of chivalry to which all knights agreed, but the same themes appear repeatedly. At the most basic level, a knight should display physical strength, excellent horsemanship, and ferocity in battle. Beyond that, a knight should be courageous. All of these attributes are to be expected of a good cavalryman. A knight should also be loyal, both to his lord and to his comrades. He should be generous. He should protect the poor and especially ladies, as well as protecting churches and those who serve them.

There was a sense among contemporary writers that chivalry in its full sense was very difficult, and very expensive. This was the value system of an elite, whose members actively desired to display their status with acts that sometimes negated military effectiveness and self-interest. Of course, many – perhaps even most – knights did not fully live up to the values of chivalry, but there was hardly a knight whose life was not shaped by chivalric expectations. Unchivalrous behaviour drew the criticism or mockery of peers, if not worse punishment.

Facing page: The knight Enrico Forzate, from the *Capodilista Codex* (1434). Impossibly slim and proudly mounted on his steed, Sir Enrico represents the chivalric ideal.

Right: A crusader and his steed, from the Winchester Psalter. Piety was an essential part of the chivalric code, often expressed by crusading.

LITERARY KNIGHTS

From earliest childhood, the knight in training was exposed to the ideals of chivalry. Certainly he would have heard tales of real knights and their behaviour. At least as important were the stories told by *jongleurs* and, by the twelfth century, a growing body of written literature. Many of the characters in these stories were historical – for example, Charlemagne and the members of his court, or ancient heroes like Alexander the Great – but the writers grafted chivalric ideals onto them, helping to create a sense that members of the knightly elite had always lived by a code that had existed since the dawn of time.

Tales of mighty deeds – the *chansons de geste* – were first transmitted orally, starting in the eleventh century. They are celebrations of the war-like virtues of knights, above all honour, loyalty and courage. About 120 of these works survive, written in Old French. They tell, above all, of the emperor Charlemagne and his court. The historic Charlemagne (r. 768–814) was a great military leader whose wars of conquests inspired later generations. But what most fascinated audiences by the eleventh century was not his defeat of the Lombards or Bavarians, or even his conquest of the pagan Saxons, but his campaigns into northern Spain against the Muslims. A whole cycle of *chansons de geste* told of the adventures of William of Orange, a cousin and 'knight' of Charlemagne who defeated a Muslim army at Orange in 793.

THE *SONG OF ROLAND*

For modern readers, the best known of the *chansons de geste* is the *Song of Roland*, which reached its final written form in about 1100. It is worth exploring how the author developed his historical theme by infusing it

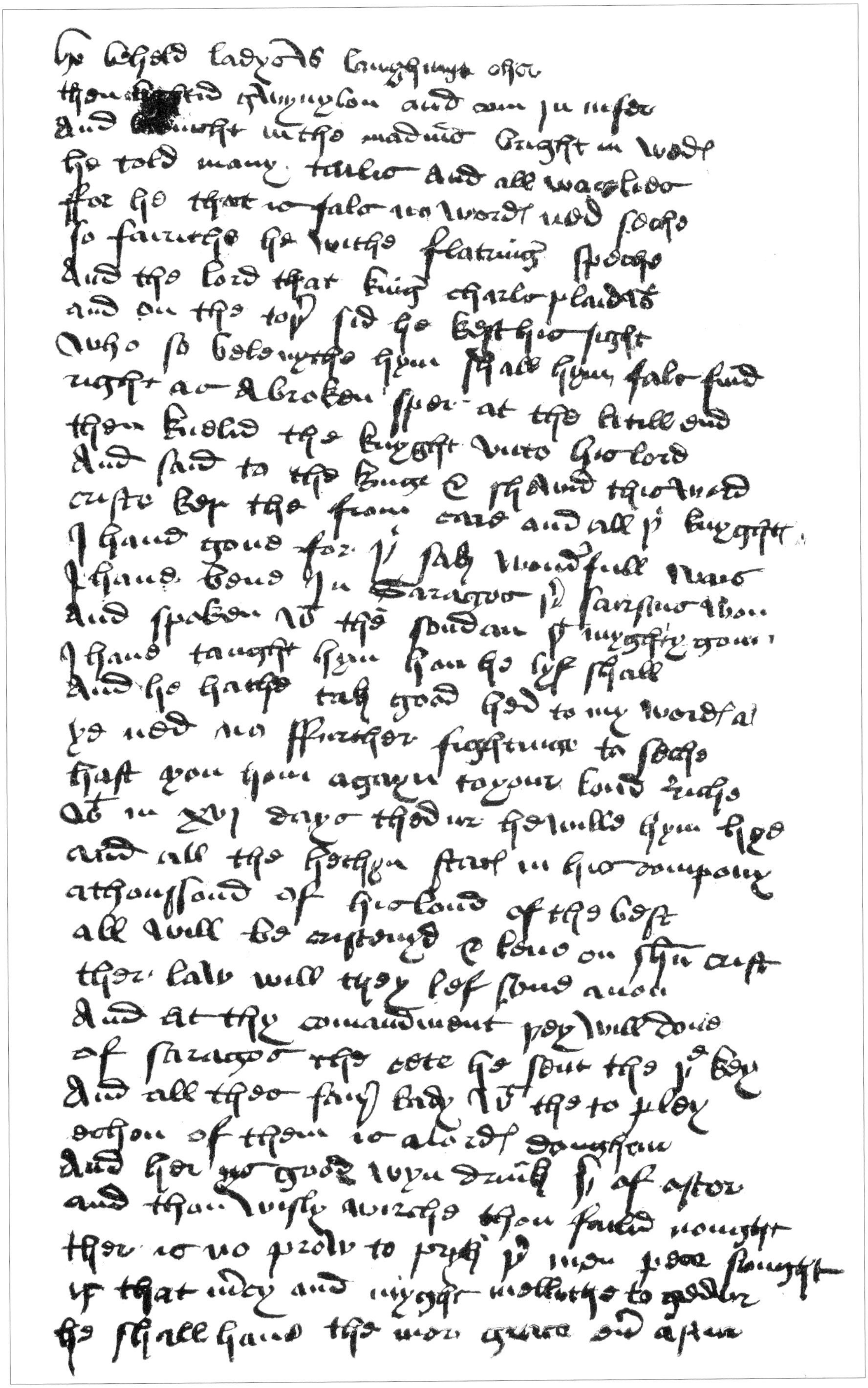

Above: A number of *chansons de geste* tell of Roland's heroic last stand at Roncesvalles. This fourteenth-century illustration catches the bloody chaos of the battle.

with chivalry, creating a story that can still inspire today. There was a historical figure named Roland, a lieutenant of Charlemagne's, who was killed in 778 when the rearguard he was commanding as Charlemagne's force withdrew from Spain was ambushed in the Pyrenees at Roncesvalles by Christian Basques. The anonymous author of the *Song* transformed this core story. Rather than conducting a fairly minor campaign, Charlemagne has fought for years in Spain, completely defeating the Muslim rulers. With the help of a traitor, the defeated 'king' hatches a plot to sap the emperor's power, manipulating events so the cream of Charlemagne's force, including his beloved nephew Roland, are placed in the rearguard as the Frankish army returns home. A massive Muslim force attacks the

Honour And The *Song Of Roland*

Perhaps the most important lesson of the *Song of Roland* and the *chansons de geste* as a whole is the centrality of honour to a knight. Death is better than shame. In military terms, central to the plot of the poem is that Roland made a serious strategic blunder – he refused to blow his horn and summon the main army back to aid the rearguard when it became obvious that a massive Muslim army was coming against them. His comrade-in-arms, Oliver, urges Roland to do so, but Roland is unwilling to appear cowardly by calling for help before even engaging with the enemy. The result is Roland's own death and that of his companions; he only winds the horn at the end of the engagement, so Charlemagne will come to avenge them and give their bodies a Christian burial. Roland's decision was not sound militarily, but it won him eternal glory. Throughout the high and later Middle Ages, pilgrims would visit the relics of Roland and his comrades, lovingly preserved at a number of monasteries in the Pyrenees, and would tell the tale of their great deeds with admiration.

isolated rearguard, eventually slaughtering them to a man.

The author paints a compelling picture of chivalry. First and foremost, to be chivalrous, one must be a Christian; there are frequent references to Muslim fighters who would be great knights if only they were Christian. Roland and his companions are represented as heroes of the faith, whose reception into heaven is assured because they are fighting the enemies of God. They are loyal, standing by each other even when they know all is lost, trying to give comfort to comrades even when mortally wounded themselves, and mourning the loss of comrades they love like brothers.

TROUBADOURS AND TALES OF LOVE

The world of the *chansons de geste* is very masculine, but growing up side by side with the *chansons* was a softer, more sensual, chivalric world, characterized by the love of fair ladies. This was the vision of the troubadour poets, whose art told of love and lovers. Most of the

Above: The troubadour Bernart de Ventadorn, from a thirteenth-century manuscript in the Bibliotheque Nationale, Paris.

Right: Many of the poems of the minnesinger are preserved in the *Codex Manesse* (early fourteenth century), featuring 137 poet portraits. This page shows Count Konrad von Kirchberg and his love.

"Troubadours and their songs of romantic love were enormously popular, to judge from the fact that the names of 460 troubadours... have come down to us..."

southern French troubadours (and their counterparts, the northern French trouvéres and the German minnesingers) were of knightly rank: the oldest extant troubadour poetry was written by a member of the high nobility, Duke William IX of Aquitaine (1071–1127). However, some could rise by talent, like the low-born Bernart de Ventadorn (1135–1194).

Troubadours and their songs of romantic love were enormously popular, to judge from the fact that the names of 460 troubadours (eight of whom were women) have come down to us, along with many of their verses. They won powerful patrons who encouraged and rewarded their work, figures such as Count Henry the Liberal (1127–1181), Countess Marie of Champagne (1145–1198), and Marie's mother, Eleanor of Aquitaine (1122–1204). Some troubadours wrote on other themes – for example, the minnesinger Walther von der Vogelweide (1170–1230) bemoaned Germany's political turmoil in song – but their overwhelmingly popular topic was love.

Some earlier troubadour poetry is sexually explicit, like the poem of Duke William in which he pretends to be a deaf-mute in order to enjoy the affections of two sisters interested in sex but hoping to keep the matter secret. But already the major troubadour Marcabru (d. 1150) chastises his fellows for their glorification of lust. Marcabru argues that true love must include patience and restraint. His fellow poet Arnaut Daniel (1150–1210) stressed that love inspires and encourages lovers to moral perfection.

This last point was the most enduring legacy of the troubadours. They popularized the idea that a gentleman, a noble, should love, because without love he cannot hope to perfect himself. This notion of the ennobling properties of love became part of the medieval chivalric world. Although they wrote of sexual gratification (a common genre was the *alba*, the 'dawn song', that tells of lovers parting at dawn), it was the emotion of love rather than its consummation that took centre stage.

What a true knight should do, said the troubadours, was to love a married woman of higher social status. He should strive for renown to do his lady honour, but at the same time should keep the object of his love secret. If one takes troubadour advice literally, even the lady might not know of the affection of the knight who loves her. This could sometimes rise to the level of satire; for example, Chaucer's 'Knight's Tale' relates a story of two knights duelling over a lady who did not even know they existed.

The reality was almost certainly that, for most knights, the 'service of ladies' was a courtly conceit, more an act than a reality, a device that could give knights an excuse for chivalrous behaviour. Upper-class ladies would rarely have had the opportunity to commit adultery, even if they had had the desire to do so; the adultery of Guinevere

Right: Palamon and Arcite in mortal combat, from Chaucer's 'Knight's Tale'.

and Iseult was the stuff of romance rather than daily life. Even a suspicion that a knight was paying too much attention to a lady of superior rank could be dangerous, as when Henry the Young King suspected that William Marshal's courtly attentions to Queen Margaret were adulterous and nearly killed his mentor as a result.

What we hear of most frequently is knights performing valorous acts to honour their lady, without the lady in question being named. Thus, for example, Ulrich von Liechtenstein in his tournament circuit of 1226 boasted that he broke 307 lances in jousts to honour his lady. The fourteenth-

"Even a suspicion that a knight was paying too much attention to a lady of superior rank could be dangerous..."

century chronicler Froissart tells of English knights at Valenciennes who each wore an eye patch, having vowed to see with only one eye until they had performed a deed of arms worthy of their ladies. As late as the mid-fifteenth century, we have an account that the great Castilian knight Pero Niño sent his lady the sword he had used in battle, with the blade all hacked

and worn. But who were the ladies, and did they exist at all? As modern scholars have long noted, the lady loves of troubadour poetry are so vaguely described that they are interchangeable.

Literature was clear on the proper relations between a knight and ladies, however. The part of this code of 'courtly love' that certainly entered chivalric practice was that a knight should honour and respect all ladies of his own social class or above, protecting them if necessary. Did they, however, rule on fine points of the proper relationship between a knight and his lady? Andreas Capellanus says they did, in a work he penned in c. 1190 called *The Art of Courtly Love*. In this work, Andreas describes Countess Marie of Champagne's courts of love, formal hearings at which the countess and her ladies would make rulings on propriety in romantic relationships. It was, among other points, the view of this tribunal that true love was only possible outside of marriage. Andreas' account was, however, probably a fiction and indeed seems intended as a subtle satire of the conventions of chivalric love.

Left: The romance of Tristan tells of the hero's illicit passion for his queen, caused by a love potion that the two of them drank by mishap.

Above: Dragging the Trojan Horse into Troy, from Benedict of St-Maure's Romance of Troy, the characters of which have been transformed into medieval knights.

THE KNIGHT OF ROMANCE

The genre that wove together the chivalric glory of the *chansons de geste* with the courtly love of the troubadours was the romance, so called because these works were first written in the French vernacular, rather than in the formal Latin of the schools. The writing of romances was not restricted to France, however, and we have many specimens from throughout Europe, including romances transformed into Icelandic sagas. The genre was immensely popular, and medieval romances can still be read with pleasure. Although few people would have been able to afford a library like the 59 chivalric romances that Edward III of England owned, romances were copied and circulated widely.

Even those who could not read for themselves could join the circle of people listening to a romance being read out.

By thirteenth-century reckoning, there were three great subjects for romance writing. The first and greatest was the Matter of Britain, tales of King Arthur and his court. But the Matter of France, tales of Charlemagne, continued to be popular, as authors added courtly love and gentler chivalric virtues to the older stories about characters like Roland. Finally, there was the Matter of Rome the Great, tales of ancient Greece and Rome, which transformed ancient history into marvellous tales of knightly values against the exotic backdrop of the ancient world.

The earliest romance we have dealing with the Matter of Rome is one of the earliest romances of which we know, suggesting that authors took inspiration from classical Latin tales. It is the *Romance of Troy*, composed in about 1160 by the poet Benedict of St-Maure. Unlike most later romances, it is poetry rather than prose, a sprawling 40,000-line work that tells of the fall of Troy. It inspired a large number of similar efforts, which often took minor characters from classical accounts of the Trojan War and built them into chivalric heroes.

Then there was King Arthur. Arthur, if such a man ever existed,

Above: A medieval monk hunched over his work. Many writers of chivalric tales were members of the clergy, like Geoffrey of Monmouth.

lived at the end of Roman Britain; he may have slowed the invasion and settlement of the Angles and Saxons in what became England. He is a rather mysterious figure in early Welsh literature. But in the twelfth century, Arthur was 'medievalized'. The author who deserves foremost credit for this development is Geoffrey of Monmouth, a cleric who some time before 1150 wrote a Latin *History of the Kings of Britain*. This largely fictional work took old legends and infused them with chivalric ideals, creating the very durable figure of Arthur as great king surrounded by a court of noble knights and high-born ladies.

By c. 1155, the Norman poet Wace adapted Geoffrey's account into the first romance of Arthur, the *Roman de Brut*. Wace's poem includes the first mention of a Round Table, where the cream of Arthur's knights enjoyed equality with each other and formed a chivalric brotherhood.

THE INFLUENCE OF CHRÉTIEN DE TROYES

The Arthurian romance burst into full flower with the works of Chrétien de Troyes, who wrote five romances between 1165 and 1190. Chrétien, who enjoyed the patronage of Henry the Liberal of Champagne, introduced several important characters and themes to the tale of Arthur, most notably the knights Lancelot and Percival, and the Holy Grail. Central to each of his romances is the knight errant –

Chrétien De Troyes' *Perceval*

In *Perceval*, Chrétien de Troyes created a compelling character, a boy of noble birth whose mother had brought him up in complete ignorance of chivalry. When he first encounters knights, the youth thinks they are God and his angels. He decides to be a knight himself, and does so in the most expeditious method possible, by killing a knight with his javelin and then attiring himself in the dead man's armour. Percival soon learns, however, that there is much more to being a knight than that. His mother had already told him, before he set out into the

the knight who wanders around the world looking for adventure. Along the way, Chrétien's knights rescue damsels in distress, battle dragons, face enchantments, and so on. But perhaps more important than what his knightly heroes do is the way in which they do it. Chrétien used his romances as a broad canvas on which to paint what he believed to be truly chivalric behaviour, which in turn made his works useful to his own and later generations as a guide to proper conduct.

Chrétien in his romances preaches a chivalric gospel of prowess, loyalty and courtesy; characteristics that became standard in depictions of good knights for the rest of the Middle Ages. A frequent lesson is that

world, that he should help maidens in distress and never take anything more from them than a kiss or a ring; he should also enter and pray in any church he passes. He misunderstood his mother's counsel, breaking into a noble lady's tent, kissing her soundly, and seizing the ring from her finger.

But soon an older, wiser knight, Sir Gornemont, takes Percival under his wing. He repeats the maternal advice to help women and orphans, but adds some key chivalric rules: Percival should give mercy to any knight who asks for it, and also he should not talk too much. Percival's behaviour soon

Above: Sir Perceval being received by the Fisher King, but failing to ask for an explanation of the mysterious sights he sees in the castle (twelfth century).

improves, and he becomes a paragon of chivalry. Unfortunately, Chrétien left the work unfinished.

"The whole adds a distinctive element: the quest for spiritual perfection, without which a knight cannot be complete."

lack of moderation is a bad thing and to be avoided at all costs, a lesson Chrétien seems to have thought real knights needed to heed. At his hands, too much of even a good thing is wrong. His earliest romance is the tale *Erec and Enide*. Full of jousts and the delights of courtly love, it still has a strong teaching element. In the story, Erec marries the fair Enide and is so besotted with love for her that he stops carrying out knightly feats, instead content to stay quietly at home with her. Only when he overhears Enide mourning the change in her husband's character does he realize his fault and forces his wife to ride out with him as he proves he is still a true and brave knight.

Chrétien de Troyes' works were popular, and Hartmann von Aue (c. 1160–c. 1210) introduced the Arthurian romance to German literature by translating two of Chrétien's romances. Other Germans soon took up the 'Matter of Britain', carrying Chrétien's chivalric instruction even further.

One of the classics of the German language is *Parzival*, the story of Percival interpreted by the poet Wolfram von Eschenbach (c. 1170–c. 1220). Wolfram's starting point is Chrétien's tale, so we see in more developed form the young hero's first encounters

with chivalry and explore in greater detail the dynamic of King Arthur's court. The focus of the work, however, is the quest for the Grail, which in Wolfram's version seems to be a gemstone with miraculous properties. Early in the quest, Percival finds himself within reach of his goal, but fails to ask the key question that would heal the ravaged land with the Grail's power. The rest of the book explores Percival's redemption of his fault after a long quest. The whole adds a distinctive element: the quest for spiritual perfection, without which a knight cannot be complete. This spiritual element, ultimately the quest for redemption, became an ever more central element of romance in the thirteenth and fourteenth centuries.

THE THEME OF KNIGHTLY REDEMPTION

It is the quest for redemption that added enormous depth and pathos to the tales of Sir Lancelot of the Lake. Lancelot was a paragon of chivalry in most ways. A peerless warrior, he followed the chivalric code; one tale informs us that the Lady of the Lake instructed him in the rules of proper behaviour. But Lancelot had one great flaw.

Right: Lancelot and Guinevere falling in love, by Gustave Doré, for an edition of Tennyson's *Idylls of the King*.

Galahad: The Perfect Knight

The perfect knight of literature was not the sensual Lancelot, but the virginally pure Galahad. Galahad first appears in the thirteenth century, the son of Lancelot and Elaine. He alone was able to sit on the Siege Perilous, the vacant seat at King Arthur's Round Table reserved for the greatest knight of all time.

The fully developed character bore a white shield marked with a red cross that had been drawn in blood by Joseph of Arimathea.

He obtained the sword of King David, and also the Holy Lance that pierced Christ's side in the crucifixion. He fought allegorical battles; for example, with seven knights who represent the seven deadly sins.

Above all, though, Galahad succeeded in the quest of the Holy Grail, winning his way to a mystical communion with a wonder-working object that by this time has become the cup from which Jesus drank at the Last Supper,

Above: 'The Attainment', one of the Holy Grail Tapestries woven for Stanmore Hall in 1895–6, shows Galahad, Boris and Percival enraptured by a vision of the Holy Grail.

which was also used to catch his blood when he was crucified.

The mystical tales of the Grail quest are probably the most inaccessible for modern audiences, but their popularity in the later Middle Ages sheds light on the spiritual longings of chivalry.

He loved a lady, the object of his devotion, for whom he performed his gallant deeds. But in Lancelot's case devotion developed into a great failure in loyalty, because the lady was Queen Guinevere, the wife of Lancelot's lord Arthur, and Lancelot's devotion in time led to adultery. This was as grievous a treason against one's lord, as could be imagined. Because of his spiritual imperfection, Lancelot was unworthy even to see the Holy Grail, much less win it. Ultimately, this flaw led to the mortal wounding of Arthur and

the destruction of the Round Table, when Mordred accused Guinevere of adultery and Lancelot carried her off to safety, provoking the final war in which most of Arthur's heroes died. Even so, some versions of his tale report that Lancelot finally found redemption, becoming a hermit and paying for his sins with his penitence; at the end, angels carried his soul to heaven.

Many romances focus on transgressions against the chivalric code, their villains' unhappy endings helping to drive home the lesson that one should behave with

proper chivalry. An interesting example of this sort of inverted romance is the English romance *Emaré*, written in the second half of the fourteenth century. *Emaré* is a lurid tale of an emperor who wanted to commit incest with his own daughter, then set her adrift in a small boat when she refused his advances, following her adventures after her rescue. In general in romances, although bad knights may triumph for a time, the good are the winners in the end.

Authors continued to produce romances for centuries. Frequently,

the same hero appeared in many tales, as authors added their own embellishment to a heroic tale. Lancelot appears very frequently, as do knights of Arthur's court like Percival, Gawain or ultimately Galahad, the perfect knight who wins the Grail. Knightly values could be superimposed on very unlikely objects, like the rooster Chanticleer and his favourite wife Pertelote, whom Chaucer depicts as a knight and lady in a romance in his 'Nun's Priest's Tale'.

There was no sign of interest in romances waning when Sir Thomas Malory produced the vast *Le Morte d'Arthur* in the 1450s, a great compilation of the Arthurian legends that had appeared over the preceding three centuries. Malory's work was one of the earliest books printed in England, and rapidly ran through several editions. As late

Above: Don Quixote de La Mancha, his head filled with chivalric romances, rides off in quest of adventure.

as the early seventeenth century, the reading of romances was so popular that it provoked Miguel de Cervantes' parody of a Spanish gentleman, Don Quixote de la Mancha, who read so many that it addled his brain and he set out to be a knight errant himself.

"…the piety of knights had a central place in romances from an early stage, as when Percival's mother instructs him to stop at every church and pray."

THE KNIGHT AND HIS GOD

As we have seen, the piety of knights had a central place in romances from an early stage, as when Percival's mother instructs him to stop at every church and pray. Chivalric piety went much deeper than that, though. It was a piety that may seem unfamiliar to modern Christian readers, since there is little in it about suffering meekly or turning the other cheek.

But medieval people knew that war had always existed; the first war had occurred in heaven, when Satan rebelled against God and the good angels had to rally in defence of their Overlord. One could be a good knight – and a good man – if one fought in the right way for the right cause. Authors as early as Chrétien de Troyes were clear on this point: the order of chivalry comes from God and is the highest order that God has made.

A specifically chivalric piety was developing by the mid-eleventh century. It was based on an active, martial life, with no qualms about the pursuit of

Facing page: Folquet de Marseille (c. 1150–1231), a major troubadour who renounced his secular life when in his forties and became a Cistercian monk; a few years later he was appointed Bishop of Toulouse.

military glory. Although authors like Bernard of Clairvaux (1090–1153) frequently complained that knights as a class were destined for hell, knights were more selective in their thinking. If possible, they kept the relics of saints embedded in their sword hilts (legend tells that Roland's sword Durendal had St Peter's tooth, a hair of St Denis, and a bit of the Virgin Mary's robe), and increasingly they invoked saints to help them in battle. There is a sense, though, that they should fight for good causes and should behave honourably and with self-control.

A common theme in troubadour poetry is that worldly love can lead a knight to the love of God. Indeed, Dante tells of one troubadour in Paradise, Folquet de Marseille, who eventually became a monk, then Bishop of Toulouse.

While the typical knight certainly did not go to such extremes (the average knight did not have sufficient education for a position in the higher clergy), there is no reason to doubt their sincerity. They endowed churches, went on pilgrimage and exercised considerable discretion in the causes for which they chose to fight. Above all else, they went on crusade.

CHIVALRY AND THE CRUSADES

Without this particular chivalric brand of piety, it is impossible to imagine that the crusades could have come into being or endured for so long. Fundamentally, the crusades, that vast series of expeditions intended to win and hold the lands where Jesus had once taught and suffered, constituted the essence of chivalry. This is not to denigrate the hundreds of thousands of men, women, and sometimes children of lower rank who fought and died on crusade.

But the people who paid the bills of the expeditions were members of the chivalric class, and it was their enthusiasm that propelled so many Western Christians into these wars. In the twelfth and thirteenth centuries, it was the crusader who was the perfect incarnation of chivalry.

Already before the First Crusade, knights regarded warfare against Muslims as specially blessed by God. We can see this attitude in the *chansons de geste*, which presented attacks on Muslims as elemental struggles of Christian good versus Muslim evil. This was not just a literary device; Normans fighting in Italy against Muslims at the Battle of Cerami in 1063 believed that St George miraculously appeared to fight on their side. St George became a particularly popular knight among the knightly class, whose members believed he also supported their troops on the crusade.

When Pope Urban II preached the First Crusade at Clermont in November of 1095, his message to

Above: 'The Battle of Cerami' by Prosper Lafaye, c. 1838. In this painting, the artist imaginatively reconstructs Roger I's victory over the Muslims in Sicily in 1063.

knights was simple: stop fighting each other and instead take arms in support of a worthy cause. Not only were Muslims oppressing the Christians of the East, they were dishonouring the most holy places of Christianity, those associated with the life of Christ. Those

assembled joined in shouts of 'God wills it!' and vowed to liberate the Holy Sepulchre; thousands more knights and tens of thousands of foot soldiers joined them.

An older view of the crusades is that the typical knightly crusader was a younger son, motivated

more by a desire to win land for himself than by any spiritual purpose. For the past several decades, however, a generation of scholars has transformed that notion. Above all, they have driven home how enormously expensive it was to go on crusade.

Only knights who had a good fief already, or who were in the household of a greater lord, could hope to make the journey. Knights pawned and sold their land and spent more than they could ever hope to win on campaign to make their expedition possible. Knights

saw crusading as a way to win glory, to be sure. But above all, what appears to have motivated them was a longing to avenge the wrong that had been done to Jesus Christ, defending their heavenly Lord just as they would their lord on Earth.

" 'orders of chivalry' … all produced statutes, with common themes such as the requirement that members assist each other, be loyal, honour noble women, or pray for each other."

The crusades played a massive role in shaping the Christian side of chivalry. Throughout the twelfth and thirteenth centuries, wave after wave of knights set out, not just on the massive crusades that have been assigned numbers but practically every year in bands of at least hundreds. They fought those they proclaimed to be enemies of Christ in Spain, in southern Italy, in the Baltic, and even the heretics of southern France, but above all their aspirations focused on Jerusalem.

Many of these crusaders never returned, and hundreds of knightly families were bankrupted by the crusading movement. But the honour of having been a 'Jerusalem-farer' remained with a knight for the rest of his life and shed lustre on his family for generations. Tomb monuments proudly recorded those who had fought on crusade, while some families produced crusaders every generation, all eager to emulate the glory of their crusading forebears.

ORDERS OF CHIVALRY

Knights would always have formed close ties to chosen comrades, but the teachings of chivalry inspired some rulers to take matters a step further in the later Middle

Ages. Their inspiration was King Arthur's Round Table, or more precisely the knights (either 50 or 150 depending on the story) who sat around that table as a band of brothers, vowed to support their king and each other, united in a common cause. They also had as a model the military religious orders, the knights of which took permanent vows to live and fight together in the cause of Christianity.

Rulers plainly hoped to use chivalric inspiration to encourage their knights to ever-greater achievements, especially on the field of battle. A number of these 'orders of chivalry' were founded in the fourteenth and fifteenth centuries, intended for secular knights. They all produced statutes, with common themes such as the requirement that members assist each other, be loyal, honour noble women, or pray for each other.

The first princely order of chivalry was the Order of the

Right: A vision of the Holy Grail appears to the knights of the Round Table, initiating the Quest of the Grail. Note that Galahad holds the seat of honour; Arthur is depicted as equal to all the other knights.

Band, founded by Alfonso XI of Castile in c. 1330. Alfonso was a warrior king, who did much to strengthen royal power as well as lead onslaughts against the Moors of southern Spain. The Order of the Band, so called because its members were entitled to wear a red band or sash, was a way to reward those who distinguished themselves in valour and loyalty to their king. Its statutes included a specific mandate to fight against the Moors.

The Order of the Band died out in the fifteenth century, but the next great chivalric order still survives today – the English Order of the Garter. Edward III had toyed with the idea of creating his own Round Table, but in 1348 founded this order instead, whose members wear a garter embroidered with the order's motto, '*Honi soit qui mal y pense*' (Dishonour be to he who thinks evil of it). This almost certainly refers to King Edward's claim to the French throne, and

the order had its start in the early years of the Hundred Years' War. Although the English had proven that they could engage and defeat the cream of French chivalry at the Battle of Crécy in 1348, Edward did all he could to encourage the knightly class, whether by forcing those with the necessary property qualifications to become

Below: King Alfonso XI of Castile (1313–1350) as depicted in the Plaza Mayor Square, Salamanca.

Right: William Bruges, Garter King of Arms, commissioned the Bruges Garter Book (c. 1430) to celebrate the founding members of the order. Edward III, shown here, wears the cloak and insignia of the Garter.

knights, sponsoring tournaments or creating this new way to honour the best knights.

The Order of the Garter is limited to 26 members, and almost all the men recognized in 1348 had distinguished themselves in the Battle of Crécy. Throughout the rest of the Middle Ages and beyond, it remained a glorious tribute to outstanding military service. Members of the order were expected to live up to high ideals of loyalty and bravery, and over the centuries the overwhelming majority of people so honoured have done so.

The first French order of chivalry, the Order of the Star, created by King John II in 1351, makes it clear that members of these chivalric orders took the honour very seriously. This order was founded to help improve the morale and effectiveness of French knights after their defeat at Crécy. Their statutes included the provision, apparently intended to stiffen resolve, that members could not retreat in battle. True to their oaths, the inaugural members of the order held their ground at the Battle of Mauron in 1352. When the English centre advanced, 89 members were killed, refusing to the last to save their lives but lose their honour. In 1356, King John II probably would not have been captured at the Battle of Poitiers if he had been willing to retreat, and if most of his fellow Knights of the Star had not held their ground and been killed.

Many other orders were created in the following century. They tended to be distinguished by a distinctive item of clothing. For example, we have an Order of the Knot (Naples), the Golden Buckle (Emperor Charles IV), the Sword (kingdom of Cyprus), and the

> "The first French order of chivalry, the Order of the Star … was founded to help improve the morale and effectiveness of French knights after their defeat at Crécy."

"One of the most important… was the Order of the Golden Fleece, called into being by Duke Philip the Good of Burgundy in 1430."

Collar (the court of Savoy). Not all orders were founded by princes. For example, the late-fourteenth-century tournament champion Jean le Maingre, who was nicknamed Boucicaut, founded his own order in 1399. The members of this Order of the White Lady on a Green Shield were 30 knights who vowed to protect defenceless and disinherited ladies.

Boucicaut's order was defunct within five years, but many other chivalric orders survived for hundreds of years. One of the most important for centuries was the Order of the Golden Fleece, called into being by Duke Philip the Good of Burgundy

Left: The Battle of Crécy, 1346. Although the English knights (right) fought dismounted, the artist has chosen to depict them as properly chivalrous equestrians.

in 1430. Like all the best orders, membership in Philip's order was highly exclusive, making it a glittering and elusive prize open only to the best knights.

CHIVALRY: IDEAL AND REALITY

Did real knights live up to the ideals of chivalry that authors extolled? We have seen that chivalric piety had deep resonance, especially in convincing knights to go on crusade. The peer pressure of the orders of chivalry also encouraged member knights to live up to a high chivalric standard. But were members of the Order of the Garter or the Star really representative of the knightly population at large? Let us turn to the era of the Hundred Years' War, when a range of non-fiction sources allows us to see historic knights in action.

Above: The first solemn meeting of Philip the Good of Burgundy's Order of the Golden Fleece, painted by Joseph Albrier.

Right: An eighteenth-century engraving of the siege of Calais (1347). French knights hover in the background, but are too weak to break the English siege.

Certainly individual prowess, including a high degree of flourishing and showing off in the name of honour, was common. 'The Vows of the Heron', a poem written at the start of the Hundred Years' War in 1337, tells that the nobles of Edward III's court all made elaborate vows; for example, one swore that he would be the first to strike a blow in the war, and so on. Although the poet was probably being satirical, there was

Facing page: In the Battle of Halidon Hill (1333), the English first employed the tactic of defending ground with dismounted knights that was later used so effectively at Crécy and Poitiers.

> *"These single combats became more rather than less common in the course of the fourteenth century; increasingly, they consisted of jousting rather than real fighting with an intent to harm the enemy."*

truth behind the fiction. The first blows struck in the war were by Walter Manny, who made his own personal expedition to France in 1338 with only 40 men-at-arms, because he had vowed to be the first to strike a blow in the war.

Despite the needs of the military situation, single combat was honoured. For example, in 1333, the Battle of Halidon Hill began with a single combat, an English champion calling out and defeating a Scot. These single combats became more rather than less common in the course of the fourteenth century; increasingly, they consisted of jousting rather than real fighting with an intent to harm the enemy. More seriously, sometimes commanders considered letting champions fight instead of committing all their troops to battle. This occurred in Brittany in 1351 with the Fight of the Thirty, when the local French commander challenged the English to a fight with thirty knights on each side. Again, before the Battle of Poitiers in 1356, a French commander suggested that one hundred men on each side fight, the rest of the army viewing the event as spectators (although in this case the combat did not take place).

Fighters on both sides of the Hundred Years' War valued bravery, even courage that seems foolhardy by modern standards. A case in point is King John of Bohemia's participation in the

Battle of Crécy (1346) despite the fact that he was blind. When John's dead body was found on the field after the battle, the Prince of Wales was so struck by the man's courage that he adopted John's motto and coat of arms for himself – both are still held by the Prince of Wales.

Real knights could be both chivalric and sensible. A good example is Geoffroi de Charny (1300–1356). He was a chivalric theorist, writing three books on the subject of chivalry to further his dream to renew and reform French knighthood. In these works, especially the *Book of Chivalry*, Geoffroi expresses high ideals, such as the role of knights to keep the peace and to support the world's divinely sanctioned social structures. He also said that any knight who failed to make a name for himself should have his teeth pulled out one by one. But Geoffroi de Charny also practised what he preached. He was a famous knight both in tournaments and in war, and had the honour of carrying the French royal standard, the Oriflamme, in the Battle of Poitiers, where he died in its defence.

HONOURING THE ENEMY

It was at the Battle of Poitiers in 1356 that King John II of France was captured, and the capture demonstrates the chivalric code at work among both the French and the English. John, the founder of the Order of the Star, refused to retreat from the battle. Even when overwhelmed, he refused to yield to an inferior, until an Englishman agreed to accept his surrender on behalf of the Black Prince, who was in command of the English force. Prince Edward then treated his captive with signal courtesy, waiting on him at table and later conveying him to honourable captivity in London.

Although it made military sense to keep John for life, Edward III agreed to ransom him – after all, one should treat enemy knights with mercy and courtesy. John was in fact released when only part of his ransom had been paid; then when further payment was delayed, he voluntarily returned to England, unwilling to break his sworn word. He died in England before the rest of the ransom was raised.

Although increasing numbers of knights died on the battlefields

well, but this forbearance did not extend to members of the lower class. Much of the Hundred Years' War consisted of devastating raids directed against the peasants of France. The wanton destruction of these raids was not considered a chivalric breach; after all, as Henry V of England said, 'war without fire is like sausages without mustard.'

The Black Prince was personally guilty of deeds that by modern standards are war crimes, most notably the sack and massacre he ordered at Limoges in 1370. Yet still Chandos Herald in his *Life of the Black Prince* felt able to hold the prince up as an ideal chivalric hero without any sense of irony. After all, he did not target nobles. When in the heat of the Battle of Agincourt (1415) Henry V ordered the execution of prisoners, his knights refused to carry out the deed because it would be dishonourable (even though it was a military necessity); the king had to turn the job over to archers, who clubbed the enemy knights to death.

Ruses of war were not considered a breach of the chivalric code. For example, the French knight Bertrand du Guesclin was hailed as a paragon of chivalry, yet

of the Hundred Years' War compared to earlier centuries, captive knights were usually treated well. We know of one Frenchman, Raoul de Tancarville, who was captured by Englishmen in 1347 and on his return to France

praised his captors so much that the exasperated French king had him executed.

The Black Prince's treatment of King John, however, brings up an important issue: knights were expected to treat other nobles

early in his career he took a castle by disguising himself and some of his followers as peasant women to get into the place. In the Anglo-Scottish wars, Sir James Douglas assaulted the English garrison in Douglas Castle on Palm Sunday when they were all in church. Even more famously, Robert the Bruce made a speciality of sneaking into enemy-held fortresses in the dead of night. Edward I in particular responded vigorously, among other deeds capturing Robert's sister and the countess of Buchan and displaying them in cages at Berwick and Roxburgh. Yet neither ruler was ever accused of unchivalrous behaviour.

Right: Bertrand du Guesclin, depicted here as a tenth 'Worthy' – fit to stand with the Nine Worthies of legend as a perfect knight.

Right: In the Battle of Patay (1429), French knights charged the English army before their longbowmen were entrenched; the result was a humiliating English defeat.

BREACHING THE CHIVALRIC CODE

Perhaps the best evidence that knights did indeed live by a chivalric code is when we see that code breached. A knight who committed treason was not only executed but dishonoured: his coat of arms was stripped off, the spurs hacked from his feet, his sword was broken, and his arms were reversed. When a knight committed a lesser offence he could also face dishonour. For example, a Knight of the Garter, Sir John Fastolf, was part of the defeated English army at the Battle of Patay in 1429. He was one of the few to escape the field – and was stripped of the Order of the Garter because his actions were adjudged shameful. Fastolf in general was regarded as unchivalric. For example, unlike the magnanimous Bertrand du

Guesclin, the Englishman became rich by investing the profits of war, winning a reputation for greed.

A prime location to shame an unknightly knight was at a tournament. By the end of the fourteenth century, entry in a tournament included a morals test, and knights whose behaviour

was deemed scandalous were turned away, even great nobles; in 1434, the Duke of Bavaria was denied entry in a tournament because he was conducting a scandalous affair.

The life of most knights was a balancing act. A knight would have tried to show his prowess, but remained conscious that he should apply his strength and skill to worthy goals. He should have high courage but also be able to control his impulses. The honour he showed ladies should be cautious and never go too far. He should show generosity and magnanimity towards enemies, but should also have the wisdom not to behave in a foolhardy way that would endanger his comrades or the cause for which he was fighting. The rules for proper conduct that chivalry imposed guarded Europe from chaos; they also provided the knight – and the society around him – with ideals to cherish.

Training and Fighting Techniques

By the twelfth century, except in Italy, it had become unusual for anyone to become a knight but the son of a knight. But knighthood was far from being an honour automatically granted when a noble boy came of age. The candidate for knighthood had to prove real military prowess. He required the ability to control a mettlesome stallion, even if his steed was panicked or wounded.

The prospective knight had to be able to handle a heavy lance, keeping it steady while charging at a gallop and holding it firmly enough to unseat an enemy who was careening towards him at the same breakneck speed. He had to be able to bear the weight of 18–32kg (40–70lb) of armour (depending on the period), the suffocating heat of battle, and the gruelling muscle burn of fighting with a sword, sometimes for hours at a stretch. Such abilities and endurance could only be gained with long and frequently painful training. So, from childhood, the prospective knight was trained for feats of arms.

THE BOYHOOD OF A KNIGHT

The boys of noble families spent the first seven years of their lives mostly under their mothers' care. But even in young childhood, the future knight would have been conditioned for the life to which he would aspire as an adult. He would hear songs and stories of great knightly deeds from the time he was in the cradle, and probably would have seen the mighty deeds of his ancestors emblazoned on tapestries in his home. The boy would also have received toys that evoked the life of knights: hobbyhorses to ride or toy knights crafted from pewter. Thanks to the good records kept by the English court, we know that King Edward I gave his sons toy castles and miniature siege engines to inspire

Facing page: In this scene from the Codex Manesse (1310), ladies look on as their knights compete in a tournament melée.

Left: At the first stage of training to be a knight, young pages would have served the noble members of the household where they lived.

"...the aspirant knight would have spent time in the care of horses and working with a trainer at increasingly rigorous physical exercise."

their imagination, and there is no reason to believe that the princes' toys were unique.

At about the age of seven, the healthy boy intended for a future as a member of the knightly elite was separated from the care of women. After that, his life was lived in an intensely masculine atmosphere.

Below: Much of a knight-aspirant's time would have been spent with physical training, with special attention to equestrian skills.

His first step towards the knightly life was service as a page; boys would typically be sent to serve in a noble household, usually the father's overlord or kinsman. For example, the great English knight William Marshal (1147–1219) as a boy was put into the household of a count who was his cousin. He would have grown up there as part of a pack of boys, all learning good manners by providing a range of services that included serving at table. They would have been

encouraged with stories of knightly deeds of daring, and perhaps even taught to read such tales for themselves. Above all, though, they would learn to bear arms and handle horses.

FROM PAGE TO SQUIRE
Already as a page, the aspirant knight would have spent time in the care of horses and working with a trainer at increasingly rigorous physical exercise. Training would intensify by the time the page became a squire, around the age of fourteen. Squires continued to serve their lords, but that service was increasingly likely to include caring for the lord's arms or even riding with him on campaign to care for his gear and fight if necessary.

The squires in service learned how to fight from their lord and

Above: A knight fighting the pell, a post erected in the exercise yard. Twenty minutes of vigorous sword work would have exhausted the strongest fighter.

Below: The first stage of training to use a lance, holding it two-handed and advancing against an enemy on foot.

his companions. Larger households probably also had a special tutor in arms whose task was to train aspirant knights. One such tutor appears in the biography of William Marshal. In 1155, Henry II had his eldest son crowned as co-ruler. To suit his new dignity, Henry 'the Young King' needed a separate household establishment from his father; as the boy was only fifteen, this household had to include a military trainer. The man the elder Henry chose for the task was William Marshal, who had already distinguished himself both on campaign and in tournaments.

A squire would have spent many hours in sword practice, using blunt or wooden swords to spar with his fellows or with adults. More time, however, would have been spent in endlessly 'attacking' a stout wooden post, the *pell*, to build up the muscles needed for endurance as a swordsman. The boys would also have practised running and jumping both with and without armour, lifting and throwing weights, even pole vaulting and climbing. Training would also have included archery and the hunting of a range of game both on horse and on foot.

FROM SQUIRE TO KNIGHT

The sons of kings and great lords were elevated to the rank of knight at a sort of coming-of-age ceremony when they were fifteen or so, although they were certainly expected to handle arms well enough by that stage so as not to embarrass their families. For everyone else, however, knighthood had to be earned, and many men of knightly family had to wait years for the honour. Until they were formally inducted as a knight they were mere squires, often fighting alongside knights clad in similar armour and riding similar horses, but enjoying lesser rank. In fact, in most armies of the later Middle Ages, knights received double the daily wage of their non-knighted counterparts.

A squire could become a knight in recognition of his military prowess, to encourage greater endeavours on the battlefield, or because he was in the right place at the right time. The last was certainly the easiest way to attain knighthood. When the sons of the great were knighted, they never stood alone; the ceremony was enhanced by also knighting the young man's companions. Thus we frequently read of twenty, thirty,

Training With A Lance

A special place was given to the necessary training and practice to use a lance in war or tournament. After his muscles had developed sufficiently to handle a lance, the squire had to learn to hit a target with it. To judge from illustrations found in the margins of medieval manuscripts, at first boys may have learned to hold a lance steady while walking, being dragged in a cart, or perhaps even mounted on the shoulders of other boys. Before long, though, the task became immensely more difficult with the addition of a horse, which had to be controlled – and that added vigorous bouncing – while the boy still had to keep his aim true.

Boys would tilt at rings, trying to put their lancehead through rings of decreasing size that were suspended with a ribbon; with a true hit, the would-be knight could carry the ring off in triumph. Most common for training, though, was the quintain. This was a vertical post, embedded in the ground, with a swivelling horizontal beam attached. On one side of the swivel was a shield, on the other side a weighted sack. The goal was to hit the shield squarely.

Above: Tilting against the quintain, a post with a swiveling arm that could knock the careless rider from his mount.

The real trick was that the hit had to be quick, so the rider could be out of range before the sack pivoted around to knock him from his horse. Once the skill was mastered, it still had to be practised; one of our earliest sources to mention the quintain tells that the knights of the First Crusade practised with it when the army was in camp.

even a hundred friends and family retainers being knighted with a prince. Most of these young men would have proven their worth already and were simply held in reserve, as it were, for a great event. But sometimes their choice could seem quite random. When the future Edward II of England was knighted in 1306, his father put out a call for all who were

eligible to present themselves for the ceremony at the same time. 300 men responded: the ensuing ceremony was so chaotic that several of them were crushed.

Other squires were knighted because they had fought valiantly, either in battle or in tournament. Perhaps the most interesting sign of the value it was believed that being a knight actually conferred

on a man, however, was that by the later thirteenth century it had become common to knight men on the *eve* of battle rather than after it. Already in 1167, William Marshal was knighted on the day before a battle, and we have seen how in the defence of Jerusalem in 1187 Balian of Ibelin knighted all noble boys in the town aged sixteen or above. Making knights on the eve of battle was expected to inspire them to greater efforts. It probably succeeded in its purpose, as the new knights strove desperately to prove themselves worthy of the honour they had received.

A good example of this phenomenon can be seen in 1346. Edward III knighted his eldest son, Edward the Black Prince, when he was only fifteen and taking part in his father's invasion of France at an early stage of the Hundred Years' War. At the Battle of Crécy, the king placed the newly created knight as one of the commanders of the vanguard, which took the brunt of repeated French charges. At one point, the prince's force was in great danger. However, when asked if reinforcements should be sent in, the king's laconic

"At one point, the prince's force was in great danger. … when asked if reinforcements should be sent in, the king's laconic response was: 'let the boy win his spurs'."

response was: 'let the boy win his spurs'. The Black Prince did so, his valiant deeds at Crécy serving as the foundation for his illustrious military career.

CREATING A KNIGHT

The act that made a knight was 'dubbing'. The word simply means a 'blow', and first appears in this

context in a 1086 entry in the *Anglo-Saxon Chronicle*. In essence, the act was simple: the aspirant knight's sponsor struck him a blow on either head or shoulder

Below: A new knight is dubbed by striking him with the open hand, while other knights affix his golden spurs and a priest provides a blessing.

"...a sword would be girded around his waist and gold spurs fixed to his heels before the ceremony culminated in the actual dubbing."

and said words to the effect of 'you are a knight'. The blow was ordinarily struck with the sponsor's hand, although later usage came to prefer a strike with the flat of a sword. Until the mid-fourteenth century, dubbing (also known as an accolade) was only carried out in England and France.

On the field of battle, the creation of a knight remained that simple – a blow and perhaps a few words of counsel from the sponsor. In times of peace, however, becoming a knight involved an elaborate ritual, intended to reinforce the ethical ideals of chivalry. By the time the ceremony was fully developed in the fourteenth century, it was imbued

with a great deal of religious content, and indeed in the thirteenth century it became common to create knights in churches. Before knighting, the aspirant would confess his sins to a priest. A bath was prepared for him, evocative of his baptism. He would then spend the night before the ceremony in a vigil, often in a church and often watching over the armour he would don the next day. On the morning of the ceremony he would hear a sermon, and then the dubbing itself would take place before the church's altar.

Below: In 1394 Richard II of England visited Ireland and knighted the kings of Connaught, Ulster, Thomond, and Leinster.

The Symbol Of The Golden Spurs

Golden spurs became the most distinctive marker of a knight. From their start as a practical device to control a powerful stallion in the heat of battle, spurs had become so inseparable from knighthood in the popular imagination that, as we have seen, Edward III could speak of his son as 'winning his spurs'. In 1302, when the Flemish urban militias defeated an army of French knights at Courtrai, killing many knights in the process, they celebrated their victory by offering the 500 pairs of knights' spurs taken from the dead at a nearby church, an act that gave the engagement the alternative name 'Battle of the Golden Spurs'.

Above: This nineteenth-century wood engraving depicts the Battle of Coutrai (1302).

This was an outrage against French honour: when Charles VI defeated the Flemings at Roosebeke in 1382, he took back the spurs.

The creation of knights remained essentially a secular act, and the sponsor who dubbed the new knight was almost always a layman. Other accounts emphasize the stages of the ceremony as a spiritual quest. Thus, after his bath, the aspirant should rest for a time on a bed, as a man preparing for great labours. His attendants would then clothe the new knight in a white robe to symbolize purity, with a scarlet cloak over it to mark his war-like calling. He would don brown stockings, as a mortal destined for death, and a white belt to serve as a reminder of chastity.

In the ceremony itself, a sword would be girded around his waist and gold spurs fixed to his heels before the ceremony culminated in the actual dubbing.

KNIGHTS IN ACTION

As the knight's golden spurs demonstrate, knighthood was above all associated with fighting on horseback, knights with their lances couched sweeping enemies before them in glorious charges. In the Middle Ages as now, attention mostly focused on knights as the ultimate cavalry warriors. In reality, however,

Above: The French avenged the slight to their chivalry at the Battle of Roosebeke in 1382.

Facing page: An artist's imagining of the capture of King Stephen at the First Battle of Lincoln. In reality, the king was fighting on foot and with an axe, since his sword had broken in the fray.

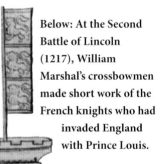

Below: At the Second Battle of Lincoln (1217), William Marshal's crossbowmen made short work of the French knights who had invaded England with Prince Louis.

the charge – or even fighting on horseback at all – was a very small part of most knights' military career. In the twelfth and thirteenth centuries, pitched battles were a rarity; even the great warrior king Richard the Lionheart of England only fought three full-scale battles in the course of his military career. Much more common were sieges. Knights played an essential role in these more static encounters, but rarely as horsemen. Mounted assaults against walls and ditches are simply impossible, although they sometimes happened anyway, as in the Battle of Lincoln in 1217. When they did occur, they were probably motivated by a misguided sense of honour, or perhaps a pride that assumed

that knights could do anything. Normally, whether defending or attacking a fortified place, the chief advantages of including knights were not their horses but rather their good armour and their leadership. In an assault on the fortress, the knights would have led the way. They were much more likely to survive and clear a space for others to follow than were lightly armed infantrymen. Even when an outside force came to relieve a castle or town, knights might well fight on foot, especially if the besiegers had erected defences or dug ditches around their camp to impede horsemen. For example, the Battle of Lincoln in February 1141 developed from an effort to raise a siege. In the early stages of the first English civil war, King Stephen was besieging Lincoln, only to be caught between the walls and a relief force loyal to Empress Matilda, his rival claimant to the throne. In the confused fighting that ensued, many knights on both sides fought on foot, including Stephen himself, who was eventually captured.

Sometimes heavy cavalry could be useful even in sieges. The knights inside a town or castle might use their horses in rapid sorties, issuing from a postern gate in an effort to take the army besieging them off guard. For their part, the besiegers would have

"When outnumbered and protecting itself, an army did not need the mobility of cavalry but rather the stiffening provided by knights in strong armour."

Right: In the Battle of the Standard, Archbishop Thurstan provided an effective rallying point for the English in the form of a mast with banners.

used heavy cavalry to take quick advantage of such sorties. Knights were also needed to protect foragers. For example, the Abodrite Prince Niklot was killed when he attacked a group of German foragers, only to have the Saxon knights protecting them ambush his force.

As in sieges, mounted knights often did not have a significant role to play in defensive battles. When outnumbered and protecting itself, an army did not need the mobility of cavalry but rather the stiffening provided by knights in strong armour. An interesting early example of dismounted knights

fighting a very effective defensive battle comes from as early as 1138. In that year, King David of Scotland invaded northern England to support his niece Matilda's claim to the English throne. King Stephen was in the south at the time, so Archbishop Thurstan of York raised local forces

to resist the invaders. The English army was badly outnumbered, so they took a defensive position on a slope to block the Scots' way, placing dismounted knights among the archers in the van to protect them and stiffen their resolve. The archers slowed and the knights were able to turn back a Scottish cavalry charge. Within about three hours of attacks, the Scottish force disintegrated, the English then clinching the victory with a mounted charge and pursuit of the fleeing enemy.

This Battle of the Standard (so called because Archbishop Thurstan had a large mast erected with banners and a consecrated host to serve as rallying point) is a useful reminder: it was a rare battle indeed where knights fought alone. Sometimes it is easy to forget that knights were part of integrated forces, serving with infantrymen of lower rank who played an essential role in battles. After all, most

narrative sources of the Middle Ages were written both by and for aristocrats, so in their descriptions of war they focus on the activity of nobles. Art too stressed the glories of knights in shining armour on horseback. In one of the most striking examples of this prejudice, the Bayeux Tapestry's portrayal of the Battle of Hastings in 1066 almost completely ignores the Norman archers, although they played a key role in winning the Norman victory.

ON THE FIELD OF BATTLE

Knights truly came into their own when they could fight in an offensive battle, an event that might happen only once or twice in their lives – or not at all. From the eleventh until at least the middle of the fourteenth century, the knights of royal households continued to form the core of the army. All kings and great lords retained household knights; typically 35 to 50 of them would actually live at court, while others could be summoned for duty when needed. It was four of Henry II's household knights who killed Archbishop Thomas Becket in his cathedral in 1170. Henry's grandson, King Henry III, could muster at least a hundred household knights in an emergency.

Kings could also call upon the feudal levies of their kingdoms: the knights who were obligated to provide military service in return for the fief they held. The rulers' right to such service was limited both by custom and frequently by written contract. Most typically, the knight was duty-bound to serve for forty days without pay.

Such service often proved to be of limited value, as by the twelfth century campaigns tended to get longer and longer or, in the case of the English kings, were fought overseas. In this age of sieges, kings needed service for longer terms and often had much greater need of infantrymen – who had to be paid – than of knights.

Except in the Kingdom of Jerusalem, where the fief-holders were expected to be in a state of constant military preparedness and could have their fiefs seized if they failed to muster with the army, it soon became the custom for rulers to accept a payment from fief-holders instead of their service in the field. This payment, called scutage ('shield money'), could then be used to finance the sort of army a particular campaign actually required. Most knights in their prime continued to take part in war, but were ordinarily paid, although at a higher rate than non-knights. Feudal levies, when summoned, brought fewer and fewer knights to the king's standard. The Capetians of France last issued a feudal summons in 1272. England persisted rather longer, but when Edward I summoned a feudal host in 1300 only 40 knights and 366 sergeants responded to the call.

Knights fought in small tactical units, most often family groups or the household of a particular lord. A knight might also be given the honorific rank of banneret for prowess in battle, which entitled him to a square flag instead of the rectangular pennons typical of knights, and the command of twenty or so

Facing page: The murder of St. Thomas Becket (1170) in Canterbury Cathedral by knights belonging to King Henry II's household.

> *"…most narrative sources of the Middle Ages were written both by and for aristocrats, so in their descriptions of war they focus on the activity of nobles."*

knights. Often the royal household had a disproportionate number of bannerets, so individual knights who were recruited for a campaign could be placed under the command of somebody with greater military experience. For example, Edward II of England's household included 32 bannerets and 89 ordinary knights. These small units – known as *conrois* – could be sent in succession against an enemy position, be sent to protect convoys, and so on, giving a well-directed cavalry force considerable flexibility in battle.

"The result was gruelling, shocking encounters that must have left psychological scars on knights even though relatively few knights died in battle before the fourteenth century."

BATTLEFIELD TACTICS

On the battlefield, the mounted knight potentially carried out two main tasks, which can be summed up as charge and pursuit. An initial charge would be conducted with couched lances, a manoeuvre that was most effective when sweeping down on unprotected infantry, then after the initial charge fighting with the sword or occasionally mace or axe. Most casualties in medieval battles occurred during the pursuit of a broken enemy, as running men were unable to defend themselves from the knights riding them down as they fled.

Although some battles were a matter of a single quick charge and then pursuit, a hopelessly overmatched enemy

Above: Assault on Emperor Otto IV's standard in the Battle of Bouvines (1214). Otto was only saved from death or capture by the efforts of his household knights.

Left: A knight 'banneret' was not a hereditary office, but rather a title given to an individual with good leadership skills. It was marked by a square banner, to be followed on the battlefield.

usually avoided a pitched battle. Therefore, except in the case of surprise attack or ambush, most battles were waged between fairly equal competitors. The result was gruelling, shocking encounters that must have left psychological scars on knights even though relatively few knights died in battle before the fourteenth century.

Almost all battles of the high and late Middle Ages were fought with a combination of heavy

cavalry and infantry. Infantry came into greater prominence in the fourteenth century, as we will see, but at no point could armies do without them. Archers or spearmen could slow an enemy charge, protect the flank, or provide the anvil against which the cavalry could strike and hold the enemy. Knights would often take positions to protect infantrymen, and the reverse was also true. For example, in the Battle of Bouvines in 1214,

some of the allied force, under heavy French attack, made a circle of pikemen. Their knights would take shelter within the infantry circle to regroup, then leave to fight again. The device ultimately failed, but certainly extended the resistance of the allied army.

A battle could take hours, with the knights of the offensive army repeatedly attacking a stationary, defensive enemy, then drawing off to catch their breath, regroup, and

Above: The artist's depiction of the Battle of Falkirk (1298) gives a good impression of how overwhelming a mounted charge could be to infantrymen.

Facing page: The submission of Saxon rebels to the German Emperor Henry IV after his victory at Unstrut.

nerve themselves to charge again. A classic case of this process is the Battle of Hastings in 1066, which lasted most of a day. In a long series of attacks, Duke William of Normandy sent archers forward to thin the ranks of the Anglo-Saxon shield wall, then repeatedly charged at the head of his knights to probe for weak points in the line. At Hastings, the fighting was often desperate. Duke William had two horses killed under him and at one point in the battle his troops panicked because a rumour spread

that he himself had been killed. It was only when the Norman cavalry finally penetrated the English shield wall that they were able to win the day; an individual infantryman fighting on his own was no match for a knight on horseback.

Edward I of England won the Battle of Falkirk in 1298 in similar fashion. In that battle, the Scottish infantry took up protective positions in dense circles of pikemen known as *schiltrons*. The Scottish cavalry fled the field

at an early stage, leaving their countrymen to endure what was in effect a short, bloody siege: English longbowmen shot at them, then waves of infantry and cavalry assaults gradually exhausted them.

As the panic induced by the supposed death of William the Conqueror shows, battles could be hideously confusing. A knight would of course wear a helmet, ranging over time from a simple conical helm with a nasal guard to a great helm that completely covered the head, leaving only slits to peer through and a real danger of suffocation when overheated. Both visibility and hearing would have been severely restricted, increasing the possibility that a knight could venture too far from his comrades and become stranded in a sea of the enemy, or might even attack fighters on his own side. After all, except for town militias, armies did not usually wear uniforms. Although by the thirteenth century, knights would have borne heraldic devices on their armour, they would still have been hard to recognize in the middle of an engagement if one had been turned around.

It is a common device in romances that in the midst of battle, perhaps blinded by sweat or wounds, heroes would grievously injure their own beloved comrades. This must also have happened in reality. Dust or sometimes mud could also add to the confusion. A case in point is the Battle of Unstrut

Facing page: The Second Battle of Dorylaeum in 1147, fought in the rocky uplands of Turkey, annihilated Conrad III's army of German crusaders.

"The great danger in battle was a failure of discipline, often by men in the midst of an engagement who could not see the larger movements of the enemy."

in June 1075, a battle in which Henry IV of Germany triumphed over an army of rebellious Saxons. The battle was fought in thick dust, which led to such great confusion that some fighters on both sides fled and some units attacked men on their own side.

FAILURES IN BATTLE DISCIPLINE

The great danger in battle was a failure of discipline, often by men in the midst of an engagement who could not see the larger movements of the enemy. Commanders did their best to convince the knights under their command, for example, to wait for the sounding of a trumpet before launching an attack, but a combination of excitement and notions of chivalric honour occasionally led to premature charges. This was the moment of greatest peril for an army. Sometimes the spontaneous charge could sweep the army to victory, but often it opened a hole in the army's ranks that the enemy could exploit, as well as making the knights involved more vulnerable as they lost their tight formation while galloping after the enemy.

Some of the worst defeats in the Middle Ages were caused by

knights who failed in discipline. A particular temptation was the feigned retreat. It took a skilled commander and well-disciplined cavalrymen to execute this dangerous manoeuvre, pretending to be defeated and then regrouping and turning to engage the foe, who with luck had taken the bait and broken ranks to begin a pursuit.

William the Conqueror successfully carried out a feigned retreat at Hastings, after a real panic that he had managed to halt had inspired him to make the attempt. At Hastings it was infantrymen who took the bait, but the results could be even more devastating with knights.

A classic example is the Second Battle of Dorylaeum in 1147, when the crusading army of Emperor Conrad III fought a multi-day engagement with the Seljuk Turks. The key to the eventual Turkish victory was a simulated flight that drew out the Christian knights in pursuit, allowing the Turkish warriors to fight them on more equal terms and leaving the crusader infantry without cavalry protection. Only about a tenth of the German army survived the engagement.

Ceasing to fight too soon, before the battle was actually won, was also a spectre that must have haunted the experienced medieval commander. Repeatedly we hear of cavalrymen overrunning an enemy camp and then plundering instead of returning to the battle. In 1099, the patriarch of Jerusalem before the Battle of Ascalon even threatened to excommunicate anyone who looted without leave. More justifiable, perhaps, was when a force of knights broke the section of the enemy army they faced and rode in pursuit, thinking they were clinching victory in the process. It was in this way that England's rebellious barons won the Battle of Lewes in 1264. The royal force was initially successful in the battle, with Prince Edward routing the enemy in an effective cavalry charge. The prince and his men pursued the fleeing enemy, leaving King Henry III and the rest of the army to be soundly defeated by the rest of the baronial force and only returning after the battle was over. It took an able and experienced commander to hold his triumphant knights together and bring them back to the battlefield.

Sometimes there was a failure of discipline plain and simple, when lords committed their knights to reckless charges despite orders to hold their position, motivated by lust for glory or perhaps thinking there was an opportunity to exploit. It was such a failure of discipline that caused the failure of the first crusade of Louis IX, which ended with the capture of the king himself and most survivors of the crusading army. In the Battle of al-Mansurah in 1250, the Mamluk commander ordered the opening of a town gate as bait for the crusaders. Count Robert of Artois then, despite orders, charged into the town, where he and many of his knights were killed fighting in the narrow streets.

All told, discipline and cohesion were what counted for effective knightly combat. Nowhere was this better illustrated than in the Battle of Muret, as King Pedro of Aragon attacked a force of French crusaders in Muret in southern France. To start, Pedro left all his infantry in camp, nearly a mile to the rear, suggesting an overwhelming pride in the ability of his knights to win the day, who even by themselves outnumbered the crusaders. The crusaders under the experienced Simon de Montfort marched out of the town to confront the Aragonese. The result was a resounding defeat for the Spaniards.

> *"Repeatedly we hear of cavalrymen overrunning an enemy camp and then plundering instead of returning to the battle."*

Facing page: The first crusade of St. Louis (also known as the Seventh Crusade) ended in catastrophe at al-Mansurah, the Mamluks executing many captive Christians and holding King Louis himself for an enormous ransom.

Right: The Battle of Muret (1213) was a chaotic melée in which the organisation and discipline of the crusaders under Simon de Montfort were able to triumph.

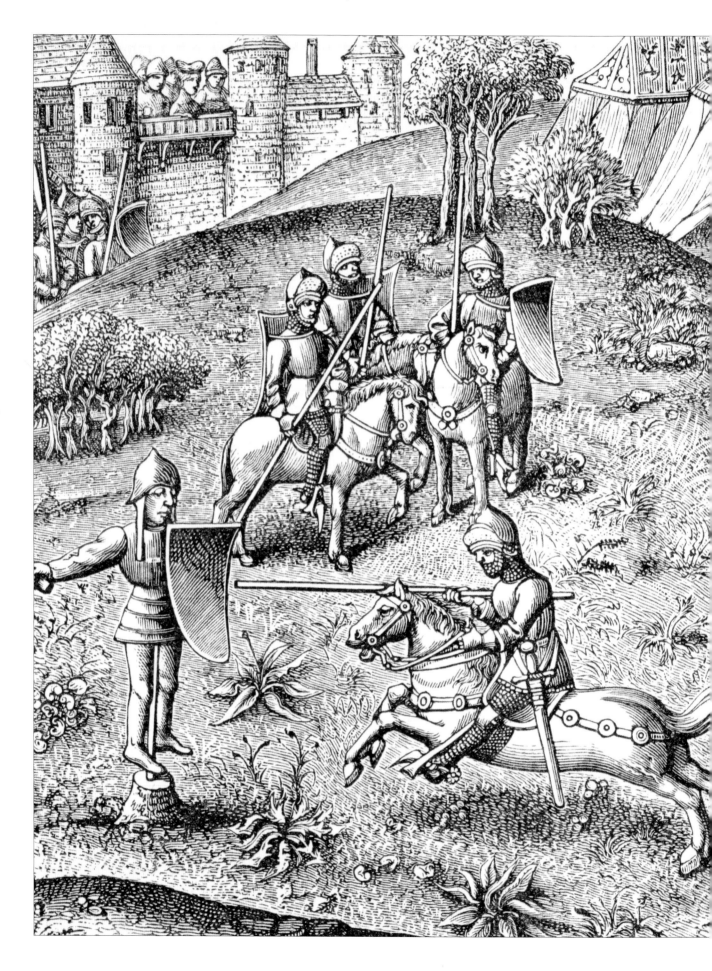

The crusaders were effectively led, charging in waves as commanded. Pedro's force was a confused mob, a problem exacerbated by the king's odd decision to disguise himself in the armour of a common knight rather than displaying himself prominently as a rallying point for his men. Pedro's son, James I of Aragon, later summed up the battle: 'On my father's side the men did not know how to range for the battle, nor how to move together; every baron fought by himself and against the order of war.' At the end of the day, most of Pedro's force lay dead, including the king himself, while only eight knights of the crusade army had fallen.

TOURNAMENTS AS TRAINING FOR WAR

Pedro of Aragon's force made such a poor showing before the walls of Muret because they had not fought before as a unit. The more often knights waged war side by side, the more effective and cohesive a force they were, as we can see from the increasing expertise of the knights on the First Crusade. But in an age when pitched battles were rare, how was a knight to hone his skills, and especially how could he learn to fight as part of a team? The answer was the tournament.

Single combat specifically to improve one's fighting skills was probably common well before formal tournaments came into being. The early-twelfth-

Left: A group of knights honing their fighting skills while in camp by tilting at the quintain.

century Byzantine historian Anna Comnena tells of a French knight who boasted that he had stood his ground at a crossroads shrine, a place where knights were accustomed to go for single combat. The knight proving himself in such single combats is a frequent figure in romances. For example, Chrétien de Troyes' *Yvain* tells of a knight guarding a magic fountain and challenging all comers.

A tournament, however, was something rather different: a

> *"Pedro's force was a confused mob, a problem exacerbated by the king's odd decision to disguise himself in the armour of a common knight rather than displaying himself prominently as a rallying point for his men."*

"...the tournaments of the twelfth century were realistic training for war, and a vital opportunity for knights to practise cavalry tactics."

mock battle that replicated an army engagement in every way except that the competitors were not supposed to try to kill each other. A late source suggests that the German Henry I invented the tournament in 938; another tradition says that the creator was an Angevin knight named Geoffrey de Preuilly, who was killed in the Norman invasion of England. Although these events perhaps first occurred as early as the eleventh century, they became popular only in the first decades of the twelfth century, emerging in northern France at about the same time that the knightly charge with couched lances became common. The first known use of the word 'tournament' was in 1114 in a law of Baldwin III of Hainault. The spate of references to tournaments in the chronicles of 1125–30 attest to their growing popularity and the spread of these events beyond France. The early tournaments were a far cry from the courtly jousting encounters of the later Middle Ages, in which two individual knights would run a carefully orchestrated charge against each other. Instead, the tournaments of the twelfth century were realistic training for war, and a vital opportunity for knights to practise cavalry tactics. Instead of fighting in individual engagements, the knights fought a melée, two teams of men making mock war against each other. Their weapons were lances, swords and maces.

Above: A sixteenth-century German tournament, held in a town square. German tournaments were often less showy, organised by jousting societies instead of princes.

Facing page: This bas-relief from a twelfth-century tomb depicts two knights jousting at a tournament. Already we see the pageantry of trumpeters and heralds.

Sometimes as many as 3000 men took part. The fight frequently ranged over the countryside, sometimes overflowing into villages that happened to be in the way, although often organizers roped off places of refuge for contestants to rest. Sometimes tournaments were even held in the streets of a town.

In the early accounts of tournaments there is no mention of referees, and it is clear that no holds were barred (although archery was frowned upon).

Sometimes the knights competing even brought foot soldiers to support them. These tournaments rapidly became both a training ground and a surrogate for war. Even the rewards of war could be won at tournaments – not just honour and renown but material gain, since the victor claimed the horse and armour as well as a ransom from any knight he captured in the melée.

The English knight William Marshal profited enormously from tournaments, in 1177 partnering

with a fellow household knight for a tour of tournaments around Western Europe. In ten months, the two working together captured and ransomed a staggering 103 knights. But it was a rough sport, as another tale from Marshal's life illustrates. William was adjudged the winner of a tournament but could not be found when the time came to award him the prize. He was finally discovered in the town blacksmith's shop with his head on the anvil, the smith beating his helmet back into shape so the triumphant knight could take it off.

Broken limbs were common, as were deaths. Although combatants were not supposed to try to kill each other, accidents were common in this violent sport, and a tournament was an ideal opportunity to pay off old grudges. Indeed, one English town cancelled a planned tournament in 1265 for fear of trouble between the sons of Simon de Montfort, the leader of a baronial revolt who had recently been killed in battle,

"William... was finally discovered in the town blacksmith's shop with his head on the anvil, the smith beating his helmet back into shape so the triumphant knight could take it off."

Below: Ulrich von Liechtenstein, who was so proud of his tournament prowess that he wrote a book about his ventures to make sure his name would not be forgotten.

Above: Henry II of France was an avid jouster; he was mortally wounded in a joust with Gabriel de Montgomery in 1559.

and the supporters of the Earl of Gloucester. At one particularly notorious tournament held at Neuss in 1241, reports tell that more than eighty knights died,

many of them suffocated in their armour in the summer heat. Nor was it just ordinary knights who died in these 'sporting' events. Henry II of England's son Geoffrey of Brittany was killed in a tournament in 1186, and as late as 1559 King Henry II of France died after a lance splinter penetrated his eye while jousting.

LATER DEVELOPMENTS IN THE TOURNAMENT

One can see the transformation in tournaments by comparing the career of William Marshal as a tournament champion to that of the Bavarian Ulrich von Liechtenstein. Both went on great jousting tours, but the account of Marshal's life tells of a hard-bitten fighting man, albeit one who was outstanding in loyalty and honour. Ulrich produced his own poetic autobiography, to make sure people knew of his glory; his account is a fantastic (and perhaps partly fictitious) confection of showmanship and posturing. He tells of two journeys when he made the rounds of the tournaments. In the first, in 1227, he travelled dressed up as the goddess Venus, challenging all comers in honour of his lady.

While that might be dismissed as youthful excess, Ulrich was certainly approaching middle age when in 1240 he clothed himself as King Arthur and travelled with a 'court' of six companions on a similar quest for honour. It became common at tournaments for knights and ladies to play the part of characters from romances, a practice first known from a tournament on the island of

Cyprus in 1223. Edward III of England and his team in a melée once dressed as the pope and his cardinals, and even odder costumes appeared, although many tournament participants had recourse to the tales of King Arthur and the knights of the Round Table. In the process, tournaments became a sport suitable for female spectators. For women to attend was still a relative novelty in 1331, when Queen Philippa of England and her ladies were nearly killed at a tournament when their viewing stand collapsed. But it added to the courtly presentation of the event to have ladies present, giving tokens to their chosen knights or presenting the prizes.

Sometimes rulers banned tournaments in their domains, on the grounds that they drew too many knights away from the field of actual battle. For example, in 1338 Philip VI of France prohibited tournaments during his war with England, and nearly a century later Henry V of England forbade tournaments for the same reason. In general, though, the advantages of tournaments outweighed their disadvantages. Especially the English kings, concerned that their knights had fewer opportunities to improve their skills than did their counterparts on the Continent, tended to patronize tournaments, although they also worked to regulate them.

For example, in 1194 Richard the Lionheart created a licensing system for tournaments held on English soil, designating five official tournament sites and even setting up a sliding scale of entry fees. Edward I and Edward III,

"For women to attend was still a relative novelty in 1331, when Queen Philippa of England and her ladies were nearly killed at a tournament when their viewing stand collapsed."

probably England's most warlike kings, both enthusiastically encouraged tournaments, not least because tournaments were an ideal locale for lords to recruit knights for their households and for campaigns. Christine de Pizan, writing in 1412, urged that to prepare French nobles for war with England tournaments should be held in every diocese of France two or three times a year, paid for with

Church Opposition To Tournaments

Above: Spanish knights training for a tournament in Brussels, 1569.

Both ecclesiastical and secular authorities complained about the violence of tournaments. A Church council held at Clermont in 1130 first condemned tournaments, repeating the prohibition at the Second Lateran Council in 1139 and at the Council of Rheims in 1148, elaborating at the Third Lateran Council in 1179 by denying a church burial to anyone killed in a tournament. In 1312, Pope Clement V tried a different approach, writing to rulers that, in light of their duty to recapture the Holy Land, they should ban all chivalric sport, including tournaments. The reaction was a wave of protest, and under pressure from the French king the next pope lifted the ban in 1316.

Papal bans of tournaments were typically ignored, but the Church's disapproval may have played a role in the gradual gentling of tournaments. In the thirteenth century, the use of 'bated' (blunt) weapons became standard. Accounts include many more references to judges, and the area of combat became more clearly defined. Although the melée did not vanish for another century, jousts – competitions between two knights – rose in popularity. And with these gradual reforms, the pageantry of tournaments increased, as did the chivalric idealism they came to embody.

royal tax revenues. Although her recommendation was impractical, it suggests a standard view of the value of training knights with tournaments.

By the fourteenth century, tournaments were only open to nobles; indeed, having participated in a tournament was accepted as a proof of nobility. In the following century, competitors had to prove no fewer than four lines of nobility in their ancestry. Tournament registration was also a way to impose and reinforce a chivalric values system, as adulterers, perjurers, robbers and other wrongdoers were also excluded. With their emphasis on chivalry, tournaments became increasingly divorced from the lived experience of war. In Germany, where tournaments were mostly organized by tourneying societies, the melée remained popular. In the rest of Europe, it was gradually displaced by the individual joust, and increasingly jousting developed from a skill into an art.

Special jousting armour, rather than a knight's ordinary equipment for war, became more and more common from the mid-fourteenth century, helping to make the tournament a very different experience from war. Even more divorced from the battlefield was the introduction of a central barrier to jousts in c. 1400. The barrier limited injuries by keeping horses from careening into each other, but increased the sense that jousting was a formal, staged event, even though it remained dangerous. Complex scoring rules for jousts had developed by the mid-fifteenth century; for example, the best blow of all was the one that knocked the opponent off his horse and brought the horse down as well.

Still, the disconnect between the tournament and preparation for war was not complete until well into the sixteenth century. Many commanders were also great tournament champions, such as Enguerrand VII de Coucy, a famed tournament fighter who commanded French troops for much of his career and was an important leader on the ill-fated Crusade of Nicopolis in 1396.

Below: The use of a central barrier in late medieval jousts helped limit injuries from horses ramming into each other at the gallop.

Armour and Weapons

Being a medieval knight was an expensive business. Throughout the golden age of knighthood, a knight was expected to have the proper equipment for war and to be able to perform military service when required. The cost of that equipment showed at a glance the knight's superior social status; even the average knight's war gear would have cost the income of an entire village, while the equipment of great nobles was exponentially more expensive. No matter what position he held in the hierarchy, a knight needed excellent protective armour to take his place in the battle line among his fellow knights, required a worthy and thoroughly trained horse, and could not do without weapons that would allow him to inflict harm on equally armoured enemies.

The great era of knighthood, roughly the period from the eleventh to the fifteenth century, saw many developments in knightly gear. Two prime factors helped encourage this evolution: the development of more lethal offensive weapons and improvements in metallurgy. Already in the ninth century, smiths had developed a better process to carburize – to add carbon to – iron, making it harder and better able to hold an edge. Most of the technological changes significant for knights occurred from the twelfth century on, as better furnaces were developed, followed by water-powered bellows that could increase smelting temperatures. Hammer mills were in use by the thirteenth century, and by c. 1400 most armour was made using this proto-industrial process to beat out the metal. The use of water mills instead of human muscle to forge and work metal made it possible to expand production enormously by the late Middle Ages.

Facing page: This reenactor is a well-dressed thirteenth-century knight, with conical great helm. Note that he is still wearing a mail hauberk, but has laminated gauntlets to protect his hands.

Right: An idealized crusading knight on horseback. Note the prominent metal plate protecting his shoulder joint.

THE IRON MEN OF THE CRUSADES

On the crusades, the Turks called Western knights 'the iron people' because, unlike Muslim and Byzantine fighters, they wore full protective body armour. The first crusading knights were clad for battle in hauberks, shirts of mail that pulled over the head and reached to mid-thigh. The method of construction for the hauberk, also known as the haubergeon, or simply as chain mail, was straightforward. A smith would produce heavy iron wire, then wind the wire around a stick of the desired diameter. After producing a coil, he would cut along one end

of the stick, producing a number of rings. Using pliers or rivets, he would then join the rings to each other, creating in time a full suit made up of tightly interlocking rings. In the eleventh century, a good hauberk could easily contain 25,000 rings and cost the annual income of a prosperous village; in central France, the value of a hauberk in this period was reckoned at 10–16 oxen. It weighed about 11kg (25lb); light enough for a fit man to move freely, but heavy enough to provide real protection. Most of the weight hung from the shoulders, but tight belting could ease that pressure somewhat. The hauberk was worn over a padded jacket (called a gambeson or aketon), which helped protect the body from the force of blows.

Chain mail was effective. The chronicler Orderic Vitalis (1075–1142) tells us, for example, that 900 knights were engaged in the Battle of Brémule in 1119, but only three were killed thanks to the excellence of their mail. However, the mail hauberk had disadvantages besides its expense. While it provided good protection against slashing sword strokes, thrusts were more dangerous. More hazardous yet were arrows, which could penetrate mail.

Therefore, when fighting armoured with a hauberk, a knight required a shield to turn direct blows and shelter himself from archers. Early knights

Above: A medallion commemorating the great twelfth-century Anglo-Norman historian Orderic Vitalis, one of our best sources for the first half of the twelfth century.

Left: A rare example of a surviving medieval mail hauberk, probably dating to the tenth or early eleventh century.

Facing page: Reenactors fighting in full plate armour. With the advent of full plate suits, shields were no longer used except in tournaments.

typically used kite-shaped shields, the tapering dimensions being well adapted for fighting from horseback. They were made of wood and probably covered with leather, the whole prevented from splitting with an iron rim. The need to occupy the left arm with a shield, however, made handling a horse in battle much more difficult, even though the shield was also supported with a neck strap. It also meant that the knight could only make use of one-handed weapons.

A second problem with the mail hauberk was the difficulty in keeping it clean and free of rust.

"By the later part of the century, the hauberk's sleeves had been extended to the full length of the arm, and mail mittens had been added to protect the hands."

Hauberks were made of iron, not modern stainless steel, and very prone to rust in damp conditions. They had to be oiled regularly, and cleaned by rolling them in a barrel along with bran or sand. It would have been a constant struggle to keep this major investment usable, and it is not surprising that almost no medieval mail has survived.

LATER DEVELOPMENTS IN ARMOUR

The twelfth century saw relatively little change in body armour. By the later part of the century, the hauberk's sleeves had been extended to the full length of the arm, and mail mittens had been added to protect the hands. The well-equipped knight had

also begun to use mail leggings (chausses) for additional protection. Chausses could also be made of iron plate, worn by lacing them behind the calf.

One of the most significant changes in armour in this period was the introduction of long surcoats, cloth tunics worn over the hauberk. A surcoat did not

provide additional protection, but, since it was blazoned with the knight's coat of arms, it made it possible to identify him and provided an important new means of knightly self-representation.

Gradually, knights adopted new equipment styles that could quite literally cover over chinks in their armour. By the mid-thirteenth century, armourers had started fashioning iron plate guards for elbows, knees and shins. Gauntlets for the hands made out of metal plate began to replace the earlier mail mittens at the end of the thirteenth century, as did the gorget, which provided better protection for the neck. Special foot armour – sabatons – appeared in about 1320.

Armour styles were never uniform, and different regions were quicker or slower to adopt new fashions. For example, as late as the start of the Hundred Years' War in 1337, English armour was very old-fashioned by continental standards, and the knights who took part in Edward III's first campaigns wore hauberks that were not much different from what Richard the Lionheart had borne on his crusade in the late twelfth century. One should also remember that although a knight would have preferred to have new armour made to order that would conform perfectly to his measurements, this was a luxury that only the wealthy could afford. Most knights probably inherited all or at least part of their gear from their fathers or other relatives. As a result, when the army mustered, spectators would have seen a pageant of armour styles from two or three generations.

Right: William Montagu, first earl of Salisbury. Although Montagu died in 1344, he is depicted here in armour of the mid-fifteenth century, copied from the Salisbury Roll.

Protection Against Crossbows

The gradual changes in armour style reflect a healthy respect for archery, especially the crossbows that were increasingly employed, and whose construction was improved in the thirteenth century. A direct hit by a crossbow bolt could kill a knight despite his hauberk. Although Church authorities condemned crossbows and threatened excommunication of any Christian who employed them in battle, they were too effective for a militarily adept prince to dismiss. This meant that a knight needed greater protection than his hauberk could afford, especially to ward off harm to his torso. This need led to an interesting development in the mid- to late-thirteenth century: the use of a surcoat that was lined with metal plates, under which the mail hauberk was still worn. By about 1340, these small metal plates were being combined to form a solid plate over the breast, which at first only covered the upper chest but was soon expanded. The full breastplate only developed at the end of the fourteenth century.

Right: German armour, c. 1450. The best armour came from workshops in Cologne and Milan. Arrows and crossbow bolts would glance off the convex surface of the breastplate.

PLATE OR 'WHITE' ARMOUR

Outside of England, plate armour was becoming dominant by the 1330s, and the English soon followed the fashion. Called 'white armour' because of its shine (especially as the surcoat went out of fashion), more and more of the body came to be protected with moulded metal plates. By the early fifteenth century, whole suits of plate, fitted to the individual, came to be the ideal in knightly gear. From head to toe, knights were as well protected as the technology of the age could make them. By the fifteenth century, the best armour – that made by experts in Milan or Cologne – was tested by firing crossbows at it at point-blank range.

Some parts of the armour would consist of solid metal plates, attached to the body with leather straps; joints would be protected with laminated armour, separate strips (lames) of metal riveted together in an overlapping pattern that could move like a lobster shell. A fifteenth-century full suit of battle armour weighed 23–27kg (50–60lb), but was easier to wear than a hauberk, since the weight was more evenly distributed around the body. A fit man could still mount a horse unaided and enjoyed a full range of motion on the battlefield. Modern caricatures of knights being raised with winches and set on their chargers would have been unheard of for active, fighting knights. By this period, though, special and much heavier armour was made for tournaments; it was the knights fighting in sport rather than war who may have needed special assistance.

The white armour of the early- to mid-fifteenth century provided outstanding protection. It was no longer necessary to use a shield to ward off heavier blows, so shields fell out of use completely after having gradually become smaller in the course of the thirteenth century. By the fifteenth century, shields were used only for tournaments. By freeing up the knight's left hand and arm, the new armour added opportunities to employ a wider range of weapons, including some that required both hands to wield.

THE HELM

Early knights needed a way to protect their heads, and that protection was expensive, although relatively simple. The eleventh-century helmet, the

Above: A sixteenth-century German knight, equipped for tournament rather than battle. The filigreed work was pretty, but could also endanger the wearer.

spangenhelm, was a style that had been widespread since late Roman times. It was constructed of a wide iron band that circled the head above the eyes, to which were attached two narrow metal bands, one running from front to back over the top of the helmet, and the other from side to side. The open areas were filled in with iron plates. To this was added a metal piece, called the nasal, to protect the nose. This helmet was worn over a padded arming cap, and increasingly over a mail coif, a hood of interlocking chains, as well.

The *spangenhelm* was good at shielding the knight from blows to the top of the head, but left much of his face and neck exposed. As armourers and the knights they served struggled to find better head protection, they faced some basic problems of human anatomy. A knight needed to be able to hear on the battlefield, so a helmet that completely sealed off the ears was a liability. He also needed to be able to see, so at least the area of the helmet directly before the eyes had to be open. And of course a knight needed to be able to breathe, so a helmet could never cover the entirety of the head but had to leave some means of ventilation.

Helmets must have been horribly frustrating. If one wore a simple *spangenhelm*, it was possible to breathe and see well on the battlefield, but there was a real danger of an arrow in the cheek or worse. More effective protection, however, meant limiting the knight's field of vision and could even lead to his suffocation if the battle took place on a hot day.

Left: A *spangenhelm*, consisting of a simple metal head covering with nasal guard. It would probably have been worn with a chin strap.

Below: The great helm, shown here in the later conical form, provided better protection but made it harder to see, hear or breathe.

"The spangenhelm was good at shielding the knight from blows to the top of the head, but left much of his face and neck exposed."

A radically different helmet design, the great helm, became fashionable in the late twelfth century and continued in use throughout the thirteenth. The great helm was made as a single piece, a hollow cylinder that completely covered the knight's head. It had narrow slits cut, through which the knight could peer in battle, and also had air holes punched around the nose or mouth. It was worn over a mail coif and an arming cap. At first, great helms were constructed with a flat top, since they were easier to make that way, but a flat top opened the knight to dangerous blows from a mace or war hammer. A new design gradually gave the great helm a conical top, off which blows would glance. By the end of the thirteenth century, these helmets began to taper more and were gradually lengthened so they would rest on the knight's shoulders and chest and could be attached to the armour there. As a result, the knight's head was well protected, but he could no longer bend his neck.

Clearly, the great helm was far from an ideal solution. After about 1350, these cumbersome, burdensome pieces of defensive armour continued to be used only for tournaments, where the shorter duration of exertion meant that suffocation was less likely, and where in the jousts that were standard by that time one did not have to worry about being able to see enemies approaching from the side. Instead, a new innovation, probably first developed in the first years of the thirteenth century, became standard: the helmet with a moveable visor. This new head armour, the visored bascinet, must have been recognized as a real improvement, because its use spread rapidly. With a mail aventail to protect the neck, the bascinet provided nearly as much protection on the battlefield as the great helm.

Further helmet developments in the fifteenth century were basically variations on the theme of the bascinet. One style that became popular was the so-called pig-snout bascinet. The visor of this helmet was rounded or conical in front of the mouth and nose, providing a hollow area with ventilation holes so the wearer could breathe more freely, making it less likely that he would need to raise his visor and expose himself to greater danger. In the fifteenth

Left: A replica of fifteenth-century armour from Ireland. The plates attached to the breastplate with straps would have provided additional protection for the thighs when mounted.

Death By Visor

At moments of relative safety in the midst of battle, a knight could raise his visor, allowing himself to breathe freely or perhaps to shout orders or obtain a better view of the situation on the battlefield. That, of course, was the time when the knight was in greatest danger. For example, Henry Percy, the famous 'Hotspur', was killed in the Battle of Shrewsbury in 1403. He had raised his visor to breathe, and took an arrow in the mouth. In the same battle, Prince Henry (the future Henry V) was wounded in the face by an arrow. If a knight were to suffer serious injury on the battlefield, it was most likely to be with a head wound, since the most vulnerable part of his body remained the head.

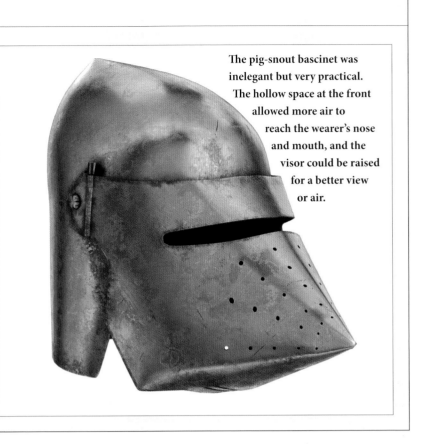

The pig-snout bascinet was inelegant but very practical. The hollow space at the front allowed more air to reach the wearer's nose and mouth, and the visor could be raised for a better view or air.

century, helmets became closer-fitting on the front of the head, for example with the sallet, a visored helm that featured a long tail that covered and provided additional protection to the neck.

THE LANCE

When charging the enemy, whether on the battlefield or in a joust, the knight's first weapon was the lance. This weapon had developed from simple spears that cavalry in the ninth century still probably threw before pressing home with swords. The spear could also be used to jab at the enemy, held either overhand or underhand; we can see both portrayed on the Bayeux Tapestry in the late eleventh century. The lance, by contrast, was thicker and heavier than a spear, balanced

"...the lance had behind it the full weight of both the knight and his horse, and in the momentum of a charge could pass completely through an unarmoured foe."

to be held at the centre. Wedged under the knight's right arm, in a charge the lance had behind it the full weight of both the knight and his horse, and in the momentum of a charge could pass completely through an unarmoured foe.

Until about 1300, the lance remained a simple pole, usually made of ash or applewood. In

the late thirteenth century, it was probably about 2.4m (8ft) long, lengthening in the fourteenth century to 3m (10ft) or even more. In the course of the fourteenth century, lances became heavier and thicker, acquiring a protective hand grip in the process. It was held angled across the horse's neck, which helped take some

of the strain off the knight's hand and arm. Still, in c. 1390, it was considered useful to add a lance-holding bracket, the arrêt de cuirasse, to the breastplate to support the lance when held in a horizontal position.

The chief effectiveness of a lance in battle lay in the force of a galloping horse, which allowed the lance-bearer to penetrate most enemies' defences. It could still, however, be used for simple thrusting like a spear. For example, in the Battle of Poitiers (1356), King John II of France rightly feared for the lives of his knights' horses if they made a mounted charge against the English positions. Therefore, he ordered his knights to dismount. They were sent, carrying their lances, to attack the English on foot. The intent must have been to have the knights trust in the protection of their armour and to penetrate over English shields or across the barricades erected before the English archers with the long weapons they were carrying. The attempt failed, but only after

Left: Eugene Delacroix' 1830 painting of the Battle of Poitiers shows King John II's last stand before his capture, his fourteen-year-old son Philip fighting by his side.

hours of bitter fighting. The French tried the same tactic at the Battle of Agincourt in 1415.

In general, a lance was useful only for an initial charge. Once a group of knights was in close contact with the enemy, its length made the lance unwieldy and impractical. The knight would drop his lance if it remained unbroken and would have recourse to a weapon more appropriate for hand-to-hand fighting. Several options were available: choice of weapon was a matter of personal taste, although whatever they preferred knights would also carry a dagger as the final weapon to use in an emergency.

THE MACE AND THE WAR HAMMER

Starting in the twelfth century, the mace was a popular option. Originally the mace appears to have been an infantry weapon, but as armour improved a weapon that could crush became desirable for knights too. By the late Middle Ages, maces were constructed completely of iron and were heavy enough to break bones and give concussions even to those wearing good helmets. It was a simple weapon: a short metal haft with a flanged head. Sometimes it was called a 'morning star', but that term was probably not used to describe a type of heavy flail linked to a haft with a chain. Indeed, there is no evidence that knights

"Originally the mace appears to have been an infantry weapon, but as armour improved a weapon that could crush became desirable for knights too."

ever used a chain mace in western Europe. The closest weapon to the studded ball on a chain that delights modern cinematographers for which modern historians have found evidence is the war flail, but that was a weapon for commoners, not knights. A chain mace would have been very difficult to use effectively in battle, as missed blows were likely to strike the user.

Another weapon for close engagements was the war hammer, which became common in the mid-thirteenth century. As the name implies, this weapon was a simple short haft with a hammer at the end, or a tip that boasted a hammer on one side and a spike on the other. The war hammer, like the mace, grew in popularity as armour became increasingly impenetrable in the age of plate. The difficulty of fighting men in plate armour also probably explains why the axe became popular again in the fourteenth century after centuries of lower-class status. An axe, thanks to its heavy head, could strike with greater force than a sword – again, a real advantage when going against knights in plate armour. The great French hero Bertrand du Guesclin (1320–80) even preferred the axe to all other weapons.

THE SWORD

The most defining weapon for a knight was his sword. By the mid-twelfth century, Emperor Frederick Barbarossa forbade commoners or Jews to bear swords, reserving them as a symbol of the aristocratic knights. By the end of the Middle Ages, in the ceremony of dubbing a new knight, the ritual

"By the mid-twelfth century, Emperor Frederick Barbarossa forbade commoners or Jews to bear swords, reserving them as a symbol of the aristocratic knights."

blow was likely to be performed with a sword (as it still is today). Long before that, girding a sword on the candidate for knighthood formed an important part of the ceremony. Swords had a special mystique. They were given names, and might well carry the relic of a saint embedded in the hilt.

A major change in sword design took place in the ninth century, producing the weapon that early knights would have used. This new design, which originated in the Rhineland, made the sword more versatile. The blade came to be tapered rather than keeping the edges perpendicular to each other; this shifted the weapon's centre of gravity from the point to the hilt. The result was a better-balanced weapon that was easier to employ on horseback.

Early knights might still occasionally have had a pattern-welded sword. This laborious technique produces an excellent, flexible blade. To create it, the swordsmith first made thin rods of iron, then welded and twisted them together, finally hammering them into a blade. The process left a distinctive rippled pattern on the blade, which gives this type of sword its name.

Below: A German mace, forged from a single piece of iron to provide greater stability.

Bottom: A German hand-and-a-half sword, early fifteenth century. A fuller (groove) has been ground down the spine of the sword to decrease its weight.

Above: A reenactor wielding a two-handed battle axe. In the age of plate armour, an axe could be more effective than a sword.

While they could be masterpieces of craftsmanship, pattern-welded swords were a necessity in the early Middle Ages if one wanted an outstanding weapon, since early medieval forges could not heat iron hot enough to work easily. If the smith worked with a single rod of iron as the starting point for a sword, the result was likely to be quite rigid or even brittle. As furnaces became more effective and new techniques developed to add carbon to iron in the forging process, the need to go through the extremely lengthy process of pattern welding vanished.

In the late eleventh century, a typical knight's sword weighed between 1 and 1.5kg (2–3lb) with a blade about 1m (3ft) long. It could be used for either cutting or thrusting. As the Middle Ages waned, swords became rather shorter. A typical knight's sword by the late thirteenth century had a 75cm (2ft 6in) blade and a 20cm (8in) hilt.

At about the same time, the shape of the sword underwent another change, from a relatively wide blade that was effective for cutting and slashing to a narrower weapon with a longer grip that was especially useful for thrusting. The reason for the change was that by this time knights were starting to combat opponents who were wearing plate armour, against which slashing strokes were ineffective. In the course of

the fourteenth century, the blade became even stiffer with a more pronounced tapering and often was reinforced, the better to thrust against plate.

All the swords described thus far could be used either on horseback or on foot. They were all intended for one-handed use, however, apparently on the assumption that, even though knights were no longer using shields, they still needed to control their horse with their left hand. A final development of the knightly sword in the fifteenth century, however, was specifically intended for use by knights fighting on foot. This was the hand-and-a-half or 'bastard' sword. It had a long grip, so it could be employed two-handed. Clearly unsuitable for horsemen, these large swords could be very effective when knights were sent on foot against a defended position.

THE HORSE AND HIS KNIGHT

By far the most iconic weapon of a knight was his horse. This living tool of war provided a knight with speed and height; a trained war stallion would also fight as a partner with his rider, wheeling and circling at a word or gesture, rearing and striking with its iron-shod hooves, biting enemy horses and their riders. The horse above all is what made a knight a knight, a member of a privileged equestrian order. Even if a knight went bankrupt, creditors were not allowed to seize his horse, as it was considered too shameful to force a knight to go on foot.

Knights cared deeply for their steeds, and warhorses appear prominently in medieval literature. For example, in the *Poem of the Cid*, the hero's mount Bavieca refused ever to take another rider after the Cid died. The *chanson* hero Renaud of Montauban had an even more spectacular horse, the magical Bayard, who could become bigger or smaller to accommodate different riders. Closer to history, an account of the Battle of Bouvines (1214) by William the Breton gives a major role to horses, the author praising them and pitying their suffering in the engagement. A main character in the poem is Emperor Otto's horse. However, the horse was also the weakest link in a knight's equipage for war.

In the eleventh century, the average horse was only 12 hands high (a typical modern Shetland pony is 10 hands). As knights moved to centre stage in the armies of Europe, an intensive selective breeding process created taller, stronger horses to bear them into battle. By the later thirteenth century, both France and England had government programs to acquire and breed warhorses, but the process of improving horse stock had begun long before that time. By the late Middle Ages, the typical warhorse stood 14–15 hands high; not a large horse by modern standards, but strong enough to bear a knight and his armour.

Horses were an enormous expense for knights, especially as they were much less durable than the knight's armour. A knight needed at least two riding or pack horses besides the charger he would ride into battle. Once in battle, the horse could easily be injured or killed, so if possible the knight would have more than one trained warhorse. In the fourteenth century, the English government reckoned that an income of £40 per year was sufficient to support knighthood, but a good warhorse at the time could easily cost £25 or more. It is no wonder that a knight would mourn if his horse were killed in battle.

To fight effectively on horseback, especially to engage in a charge, knights found several pieces of equipment essential. First and foremost, they had to be able to stay on the horse even in the shock when their lance struck an enemy. By the later eleventh century, a knight's warhorse was equipped with a saddle that wrapped part way around the knight's body, with a high,

The Destrier

Those knights who could afford to do so did not ride 'typical' warhorses into battle; they invested in a destrier, also known as a 'great horse'. The destrier had developed by the twelfth century as breeders mixed Arabian stock with European horses. These horses probably had a stocky build, more like a modern hunter than a racehorse, with a strong, short back. They were big, averaging as much as 17 hands in height. From boyhood, the future knight was trained to handle such horses, who themselves had years of training to teach them how to serve their knights.

Facing page: A knight and his horse jousting a competitor with couched lance. Medieval illustrations include many horses sporting cloths painted with heraldic devices, but we can't usually tell if there was armour underneath.

Right: An early knight's saddle. Both pommel and cantle were raised to help hold the knight in his seat; in the later Middle Ages they would actually wrap around the knight's buttocks for support.

Above: Horses being disembarked from
the Norman invasion fleet in 1066. A
panel from the Bayeux Tapestry, 1070s.

Right: Spurs and stirrups helped ease
the process of controlling a war stallion
in battle.

rigid cantle at the rear to help hold the knight in place. Stirrups, always worn long, gave extra security in the saddle.

The saddle itself was unlikely to come loose in battle thanks to double girthing or breast collars. All of this amounted to a very firm seat on the horse. Another piece of gear that was necessary to control the high-spirited stallions that knights rode into battle was spurs. Simple prick spurs were used until the rowel spur appeared in the thirteenth century.

THE CHALLENGES OF HORSES

Horses were by far the most uncertain and troublesome item in the knight's gear. Prone to injury on rough roads (although nailed horseshoes were introduced in the late ninth century) and a variety of illnesses, a horse could fail at a crucial moment. The horse had to be fed – not just grass but also grain. A horse also needs at least four gallons of water each day, and raiding parties especially could find it hard to provide for their

mounts. One English raiding party in 1355 ran so short of water that in desperation they gave their horses wine instead – and then had to deal with all the problems attendant on drunken horses.

The problems with horses rapidly multiplied when forces were transported by sea. A panicked horse can easily break a leg, and even if that can be contained equines are very prone to seasickness, their wretchedness at sea increased by the fact that they are unable to vomit. It was essential

Right: King John of Bohemia at Crécy, by Viktor Barvitius (1858). When told the battle was lost, John is supposed to have ordered his men to lead him to the thick of the fighting, where he was killed.

to develop ships that could provide warhorses with easy access in and out of a ship, for example via a door in the side of the hold that could be sealed shut before sailing. They also had to be kept quietly in place, for example held with slings suspended from beams that fit under the horses' stomachs.

> *"…archers and pikemen were purposely pitted against horses, rather than the knights who rode them."*

In battle, by far the easiest way to stop a knight was to injure or kill his horse. As effective massed infantry developed by the fourteenth century, archers and pikemen were purposely pitted against horses, rather than the knights who rode them. As we will see, English archers at Crécy or well-arrayed pikemen at Courtrai could stop a charge dead in this way. But the danger to the knight's horse in battle was by no means new in the fourteenth century. The horse was always the most vulnerable chink in the knight's armour.

"By the middle of the twelfth century, some knights used… a covering draped over especially the horse's hindquarters made of hardened leather or metal plates."

ARMOURING HORSES

Why not just armour the horses? The horses portrayed on the Bayeux Tapestry were unarmoured, but the Battle of Hastings took place when knighthood was still in its infancy. The horses suffered grievously as Norman knights tried to break through the English shield wall; the tapestry includes graphic images of stallions falling backwards down the steep slope, and other sources tell that William the Conqueror himself had several horses killed under him in the course of the battle. Over time, a variety of horse armour did develop. But several factors always had to be considered. Was the armour prohibitively expensive? Or was it too heavy, so the horse was exhausted too quickly while carrying his own and his knight's armour, besides his knight? Armour could also impinge on a horse's muscles, decreasing his mobility in battle.

Horse armour is first mentioned in our extant sources starting in the late twelfth century.

Left: Sixteenth-century plate armour for a knight and his horse. Such equipment continued to be effective in battle well into the sixteenth century.

In its earliest form it was a trapper, protection for the haunches made of chain mail. By the middle of the twelfth century, some knights used what is called 'barding' – a covering draped over especially the horse's hindquarters made of hardened leather or metal plates. Other metal plates could be used to protect the chest, while the shaffron, horse head armour, gave some protection at least to the horse's face and eyes. But it is impossible to tell how often such armour was used. For the most part, our main source of information is paintings in medieval manuscripts. But since it became the custom for knights to have their horses' barding painted with their coats of arms, we cannot tell from illustrations if the material under the heraldic symbols was metal, leather or simple cloth. Many must have compromised with barding of simple felt or leather, which would provide some safety from glancing blows but would not impede or weigh down the horse too much. Better horse armour did develop early in the fifteenth century, but by that time it had become almost standard for knights to dismount when advancing into battle.

The Charge

Perhaps the ultimate military challenge for a medieval knight was the pitched battle in which he would charge the enemy as part of a tightly packed mass of his fellows. It was for the charge above all that knights trained long and hard, participating in tournaments and mastering the use of a heavy lance.

However, many knights would have spent a lifetime in the field without ever having the opportunity to practise this skill. After all, pitched battles were rare; even when they occurred, knights were most effective at finishing off and pursuing beaten troops. Yet the mounted charge had a role – at times crucial – in the battles of the high and late Middle Ages.

In general, medieval weapons and fighting techniques favoured defence over offence, and the charge was often a commander's best hope of dislodging and defeating an enemy that had taken up a defensive position. With a massed charge, those who launched it hoped to concentrate overwhelming, irresistible force at a key point of the enemy's line, throwing the enemy into confusion and, if possible, flight. The charge relied on a number of factors, besides luck, to succeed. How well positioned was the enemy, and how were they armed? Perhaps even more important, the knights in a charge were unlikely to know how well led their enemies were, and how steadfast their resolve. Among the knights taking part in the charge, the quality of leadership was essential, especially in the decisions of exactly when and where to charge to have the greatest effect. A well-dressed line was crucial, as was the discipline that enabled a unit of knights to pull back and regroup for another onslaught if necessary. A charge could go wrong, but, until improvements in gunpowder weapons changed the face of battle, it was still the best hope for success.

THE ELEMENTS OF A SUCCESSFUL CHARGE

In the early twelfth century, the Byzantine historian Anna Comnena already recognized that Western knights in a massed

Facing page: Richard the Lionheart confronts Saladin at the Battle of Arsuf (1191). Engraving by Gustave Doré (1832–1883).

Right: Anna Comnena (1083–c. 1153) was a Byzantine princess, daughter of Emperor Alexius I Comnenus. Anna's history of her father's reign gives an important Byzantine view of the First Crusade.

charge could be devastating, describing the 'irresistible first shock' when they engaged with the enemy. To obtain that overwhelming force, the knights in the charge had to work as a team – the horses as well as the men – and failures in discipline could lead to disaster for all.

A first important element of a successful cavalry charge was that the unit of knights had to arrive at the enemy's line tightly packed. In medieval sources this is described as being such a dense formation that an apple tossed among the knights would not fall to the ground. To arrive together and with the formation intact, the horses should only be thrown into a gallop at the last possible moment. As early as 782,

the author of the *Royal Frankish Annals* criticizes a Frankish force for a stupid defeat, caused because they had advanced against the enemy at a gallop, as if they were pursuing a running enemy. What they should have done was to move forward in line at a measured speed. Modern British cavalry manuals still drive home this point, ordering that cavalry should advance in tight order and only be allowed to move above a trot when within 40 yards (36.5m/120ft) of the enemy.

The medieval ideal was a cavalry unit that was tightly packed, disciplined and trained. The knights involved had to be able to control their horses in the excitement of the charge; they also had to be able to control

Above: An idealized knightly charge, from Hans Burgkmair's Triumph of Emperor Maximilian I, 1526.

themselves, especially by staying in formation rather than falling behind or surging ahead of the line. Such a unit has a variety of names in our sources, including the *échelle*, *constabularium*, *conrois* or *bataille*. Such a 'battle', which in combat could involve hundreds of knights, would consist of a number of smaller units, most frequently 12–20 men per group, who fought as family or friend units, or often were the household knights of a lord. Depending on what was needed for the occasion, the whole 'battle' could charge together or smaller units could attack a more focused point in turn.

"...with the enemy spurring to meet the charge... simply standing and waiting for enemies to charge at a gallop was a recipe for disaster."

Sometimes charges were launched against other cavalry formations, which could lead to a massive melée on the battlefield, with the enemy spurring to meet the charge. After all, simply standing and waiting for enemies to charge at a gallop was a recipe for disaster. The use of couched lances was most effective for these cavalry versus cavalry fights; swords, maces or axes were often more useful when attempting to scatter an infantry formation.

The most successful cavalry charges were usually those against infantry. It is easy to comprehend how a solid line of several hundred heavily armoured men rushing at a gallop would induce panic in infantry. The infantryman's only hope of survival was if he and all his fellows stood their ground, since a horse will not run into what it sees as a solid barrier, no matter how much it is pricked and prodded. Of course, as we will see, the infantryman's odds were greatly improved if there were barriers to slow down and break up that solid massed charge, or if missile weapons accomplished the same purpose, so the charge wasn't able to deliver the necessary massing of force when it reached the line of defenders.

Psychologically and physically gruelling as a cavalry charge was, the most difficult point for knights and their commanders alike was if the first charge was ineffective. The fighters had to be drawn back from the fray, regrouped, and then sent in for a second – or third, or fourth – charge, picking the right moment for their onslaught to have the greatest effect. This challenge of regrouping mounted knights in the midst of battle was the ultimate test of leadership. The knights' adrenalin would be pumping, and all the stories of immortal glory won in battle would probably be going through their heads; or perhaps they had reached a state of blind, desperate struggle to survive. The high-spirited, battle-trained stallions they rode into battle would be sharing the same emotional

Below: Knights charging against tightly arrayed pikemen. Note how the charge has lost its cohesion approaching the solid mass of infantry.

overcharge. It is small wonder that the chronicles of the later Middle Ages include many tales of knights charging successfully but the battle being lost because the knights were then out of control and failed to clinch the victory.

THE CHARGE IN THE TENTH AND ELEVENTH CENTURIES

The annals of warfare provide a long history of successful cavalry charges going back to Alexander the Great and his Companion Cavalry. What made the knightly charge of the high Middle Ages distinctive, however, was the combination of close formation, heavy armour, and the focus of the knight's and his horse's full weight behind a lance.

As rulers expanded their cavalry forces in the tenth century, at least some of those conditions were met, although the proto-knights in their mail hauberks had not yet added the couched lance to their armament. Thus, already with the Battle of Lenzen in 929, a Saxon army under the command of two counts defeated the Slavic Redarii with effective cavalry. The Germans opened the battle with a cavalry charge, which failed because the horses could not

"the knightly charge… was the combination of close formation, heavy armour, and the focus of the knight's and his horse's full weight behind a lance."

manoeuvre well on the wet ground. A long infantry battle followed, culminating in a renewed charge by the Saxon cavalry reserve when a gap appeared on the enemy flank. We can also see a good example of the misused and disastrous cavalry charge in the tenth century when, at the Battle of Cotrone in 982, the German cavalry became overextended and was then cut off and defeated unit by unit by Muslim light cavalry.

The true 'knightly' cavalry charge began some time in the second half of the eleventh century. The innovators in the

Left: The ancient Persians, who fought mostly as infantry, were unable to stand up to Alexander the Great's cavalry charge at the Battle of Issus, their king himself fleeing the field.

use of this fighting technique appear to have been the Normans, although it is not clear when use of the couched lance became the norm. It is probably thanks to their effective use of the knightly charge – and their ruthless determination – that the Norman adventurers who carved out a kingdom for themselves in southern Italy and Sicily owe their success. The battle about which we are best informed is the Battle of Civitate, fought in June 1053 by the Normans led by Robert Guiscard against a coalition force determined to curb Norman ambitions, created and led by Pope Leo IX. The battle was a debâcle for the papal troops. The Normans opened the contest with a cavalry charge and most of the pope's Lombard infantry fled rather than trying to hold their line. The crumbling of the Lombard position made it possible for the Norman knights to outflank the more disciplined German troops positioned at the centre of the papal force. The fighting was hard; Robert Guiscard was unhorsed three times. But at the end of the day, the pope had become the unwilling 'guest' of the Normans and Leo IX soon recognized Robert as Duke of Apulia and Calabria.

In October 1053, the Normans in their northern French homeland also won a major victory thanks to their cavalry tactics, this time against the forces of the French king, Henry I. In this engagement, the Battle of St-Aubin-sur-Scie, the Normans were facing an army much closer to their own in composition: a mixed force of infantry and knights with similar equipment. In this case, it was the discipline of the Norman knights under Duke William that was decisive. Unable to break the enemy's lines with his first charge, William's cavalry was forced back. The French knights began a pursuit of what they thought to be their defeated foes, only to have the Normans regroup and attack them once the French line had lost all cohesion.

THE EXAMPLE OF THE BATTLE OF HASTINGS

The same tactic played a vital role in the most famous Norman encounter of this era, the Battle of Hastings in 1066. Duke William had invaded England, seeking to claim the English crown. The Norman force was met near Hastings (the battle was actually fought where the modern English town of Battle now stands) by an Anglo-Saxon army led by their king, Harold Godwinson. The English, as was their custom, fought on foot. They assumed a defensive position along the top of rising ground, well-armoured men forming a densely packed shield wall. William sent repeated charges of knights up the slope, trying with increasing desperation to break this formation. The viciousness of

Above: The armies of heaven fighting the Seven-Headed Beast of the Apocalypse; as a good knight, the king in the foreground charges with couched lance. From an Anglo-Norman verse Apocalypse, c. 1250.

Right: Robert Guiscard being invested as Duke of Apulia and Calabria by Pope Nicholas II in 1059.

the struggle is portrayed on the Bayeux Tapestry, which shows horses falling backwards after failing to break through the shield wall and William's knights lunging and thrusting with their spears to wound men over the protection of their shields. William's knights do not appear to have been using lances yet, although the Tapestry shows a few men carrying spears with an underhanded grip.

Hastings, fought so early in the history of the knightly charge, helps drive home the point that at no stage in the history of the charge could knights alone prevail against a resolute and densely formed foe with good armour. Hastings became a long, gruelling competition in which the entire Norman force – archers as well as knights – played vital roles. Repeated archery advances gradually thinned the Anglo-Saxon ranks, at some point in the battle depriving them of their chief leader by killing King Harold, who fell with an arrow in his eye. But the glory went to the knights. William was given a clue to success when a body of his knights, their charge failed, fled in some disorder away from the English. Hundreds of Englishmen broke ranks to pursue their defeated enemy, but the Normans were able to regroup and defeat them piecemeal. At a later point in the battle, Duke William purposely feigned another flight, and again was able to slaughter the

Right: The Battle of Antioch, 1098, from a fifteenth-century illustration. The crusaders with their last surviving horses have left the city walls and charged the Muslim army.

Above: A late medieval illustration of the Battle of Tinchebrai, Henry I of England defending his ground on foot while his brother's force attacks.

enemy fighters who left their line and straggled out over the field in pursuit. Finally, the Normans were able to break through the weakened shield wall, which allowed them to slaughter the individual foot soldiers and win the decisive victory that made William 'the Conqueror' king of England.

The Norman knights at Hastings do not appear to have charged with couched lances, but that technique was certainly employed by knights on the First Crusade. Most notably at the Battles of Antioch and Ascalon, the Western knights proved how effective such a charge could be, in both cases rapidly throwing the enemy army into disorder. It is this sort of charge that Anna Comnena describes, and neither Byzantines nor Muslims ever had a force that could stand up to a charge of Western knights. But were these instances true charges, in the sense used when describing the battles of the later Middle Ages?

Some scholars believe that the true, massed charge only developed fully as a battle tactic around the time of the English civil war of 1135–1154. The key feature was that the knights in the charge were trained to act as a group. At first, apparently, the knights were trained to charge in small groups of ten to twelve men; that is the most likely scenario at Hastings. But some time between Hastings and the Battle of Lincoln (1141), the concerted large-group charge became customary.

THE CHARGE IN THE TWELFTH CENTURY

Through the course of the twelfth century we can see the knightly charge becoming more and more effective – when used skilfully. An interesting example is the Battle of Tinchebrai, fought in 1106 between two sons of William the Conqueror. The younger son, King Henry I of England, had claimed both England and Normandy for himself, taking advantage of his elder brother Robert of Normandy's absence on the First Crusade. When Robert returned, he naturally wished to regain his duchy, and if possible the English throne. On the battlefield at Tinchebrai, both armies were Norman, trained to fight in the same way and well aware of their opponents' capabilities. Henry I took a defensive position, he himself joining the two lines he created of infantry, strengthened with dismounted knights, whose armour made them more able to withstand a cavalry charge. Henry's gamble proved correct, as his densely packed infantry line was able to hold its position despite Robert's massed cavalry charge. Henry's reserve cavalry was then launched against the flank of Robert's force, throwing them into disorder and winning a major victory.

Henry I adopted the same approach when he commanded an Anglo-Norman force against King Louis VI of France in the Battle of Brémule in 1119. Again, Henry ordered some of his knights to fight on foot, he himself joining their ranks. The French charge against them proved to be undisciplined and disordered, driving home how hard it was to co-ordinate an effective charge. The French were repelled and the result was another victory for the English king.

The Battle of Arsuf, fought in the Latin Kingdom of Jerusalem in 1191, serves as a final example of the twelfth-century charge. On 7 September 1191, the army of the Third Crusade under the command of King Richard the Lionheart of England was marching from Acre to Jaffa. Saladin's forces attacked the crusaders repeatedly as they marched, hoping to draw out some of the Westerners so they could be overwhelmed piecemeal. The only protection for the crusaders was to stay in close formation despite the provocation they were receiving; moreover, the crusaders' only hope of a decisive victory was to charge the Muslims at exactly the right time.

It seems clear from accounts of the battle that the English king was aware of how effective a charge against Saladin's force might be, and was waiting for the best possible moment when the Muslims could be pinned and annihilated. King Richard had placed infantry on the left of his order of march to provide some protection to his cavalry, and gave the Knights Hospitaller the dangerous honour of serving as rearguard. The Hospitallers, harried beyond bearing, launched a charge against the enemy despite Richard's order to wait. The king saved his army from potential catastrophe by immediately throwing the rest of his cavalry into a charge to support the Hospitallers, and the crusader cavalry defeated the Muslim army. But it was not the decisive victory for which Richard longed – the victory that could restore Jerusalem to Christian hands – because most of the Muslim host was able to flee.

Below: This illustration shows Richard the Lionheart during the Third Crusade in the thick of the fighting, wielding an axe.

THE GOLDEN AGE OF THE CHARGE: THE THIRTEENTH CENTURY

Three battles in close succession brought cavalry to new prominence in the early thirteenth century. In each case, what rendered cavalry charges so effective was the discipline that the knights involved demonstrated on the battlefield. This allowed their commander to use his cavalry as a fine surgical tool rather than a bludgeon, in two cases charging in repeated waves that gradually wore down the enemy.

The first of these great cavalry victories was the Battle of Las Navas de Tolosa, fought on 16 July 1212, in which a Christian army jointly led by Pedro II of Aragón, Sancho VII of Navarre and Alfonso VIII of Castile decisively defeated the Almohad caliph al-Nasir. The Christians achieved a surprise attack thanks to a shepherd who guided them through an unknown

pass to the edge of the Muslim camp. The battle was waged over rocky slopes, despite which the Christians were able to undertake a series of both infantry attacks and cavalry charges against the enemy. Although the mostly infantry Muslim army was able to hold the first Christian cavalry charge,

Left: This 1878 painting in the Palacio del Senado de España, represents well the chaotic conditions of the Battle of Las Navas de Tolosa (1212).

Above: A rare battle fought entirely between cavalry forces, the Battle of Muret (1213) helped show the world how effective a disciplined cavalry charge could be.

the Spanish knights were able to disengage, regroup and charge repeatedly. Finally, a second charge by the Christian reserve led to a complete rout of the Almohads.

The second great cavalry engagement also involved King Pedro II of Aragón, although this time he was on the losing side. This was the Battle of Muret, waged in southern France on 12 September 1213. It was an engagement of the Albigensian Crusade, as mostly northern French crusaders fought the Cathar heretics and those who supported them in southeastern France. Although King Pedro was a Catholic Christian, he agreed to support his brother-

in-law Count Raymond VI of Toulouse, especially as the king was concerned by the aggressive land seizures of the crusade leader, Simon de Montfort.

The Battle of Muret is a textbook example of how effective a disciplined knightly charge could be. Simon de Montfort, a cunning tactician, enticed Pedro to launch a direct attack on the crusader-held town of Muret by leaving one of the town gates open. The Aragonese knights and their allies (Pedro had left his infantry in camp) surged in disorder towards their tempting target. Although they halted when the crusader cavalry appeared, Pedro's men failed to dress their

A Tale Of Two Commanders

An interesting point about the Battle of Muret is the role played by the two commanders. Pedro of Aragón apparently did not anticipate giving commands once the battle had joined, or he would not have positioned himself in the second line and certainly would not have rendered himself unrecognizable by borrowing a knight's armour. Simon de Montfort, by contrast, controlled the course of the entire battle. When the time arrived for the full engagement, he was able to array his cavalry into three lines; the commanders of each line then did what he told them when he told them. He himself remained with the third line, where he could see what was happening and issue commands as necessary. When his first two lines pursued the defeated and fleeing enemy, Simon was able to halt the third line and keep his own men in reserve in case their enemy rallied and returned to the fight. Simon de Montfort was the model of the new cavalry commander of the thirteenth century.

Right: Simon de Montfort the Elder (c. 1175–1218), here shown in fifteenth-century armour, was the elected leader of the Albigensian Crusade.

Left: Philip II Augustus of France was in the thick of the fighting at the Battle of Bouvines; his leadership helped turned the tide of the battle.

lines sufficiently. Simon de Montfort then launched two waves of knights against Pedro, whose own lines were kept stationary rather than riding out in a counter-charge. The crusaders broke through both lines of Pedro's army, while simultaneously Simon led a third wave of knights to outflank the Aragonese cavalry on their left. The result was catastrophic for the Aragonese. King Pedro himself, who had made the inexplicable decision to fight disguised as an ordinary knight, was killed, as were many of his men.

The third great cavalry engagement of the early thirteenth century was fought on 27 July 1214. The Battle of Bouvines was one of the most decisive battles of the Middle Ages, led on the one side by King Philip II Augustus of France and on the other by the German Emperor Otto IV. Otto had invaded the county of Flanders with a coalition force, intending to catch the French force between his own army and that of his ally, King John of England. Each side brought about 1400 knights to the field, while Philip had between 5000 and 6000 infantry to Otto's 7500.

In three hours of vicious fighting, the French won a complete victory, owed above all to the discipline of their knights. The battle opened on the allied left flank, when a group of French light cavalrymen attacked Otto's knights in hope of sowing confusion. These French horsemen, lacking the heavy armour of knights, were soon either killed or driven back. Some of the allied knights proceeded to chase them, only to suffer the devastating charge of a contingent of French knights. In the centre, an allied charge including both cavalry and infantry led by Emperor Otto made great headway against the French urban militiamen, breaking through to King Philip and nearly killing him. But then the French knights began a long series of small cavalry attacks, gradually sapping the strength of the allied cavalry. Otto led the rest of his army in a massive but disordered charge; the result was a gigantic melée in which the discipline of the French knights gradually turned the tide.

Modern historians tend to stress the fact that Emperor Otto had relatively few men who were personally loyal to him in his coalition army, whereas Philip of France's knights were a much more cohesive force. The allied right held out longest, Count Reginald of Boulogne using a circle of pikemen as a refuge from which he and his men rode out in repeated small charges. This formation was overrun only long after the rest of the allied army was in full retreat. King Philip soon halted pursuit of the enemy because night was approaching. He recalled his knights with trumpet blasts, again displaying how well he was able to control his troops.

HEAVY CAVALRY IN THE THIRTEENTH CENTURY

After Las Navas de Tolosa, Muret and especially Bouvines, few would have questioned the military doctrine that it was effective cavalry charges that won battles. To be sure,

Below: The defeated King Henry III, abandoned on the battlefield of Lewes by his son's cavalry force, is taken captive by the rebel leaders.

Above: The Battle of Benevento (1266). As is common in medieval manuscript illuminations, the artist has left out the common footsoldiers who made up the bulk of Manfred's army.

> *"Even in the golden days of the thirteenth century, the knightly charge was not a guarantee of success because so many factors were involved."*

cavalry charges did not always work out. For example, in the Battle of Lewes (1264), Prince Edward of England successfully broke the rebel right flank with a cavalry charge, but then he and his men chased their fleeing enemies for four hours. When the prince finally returned to the battlefield, he discovered that his father, King Henry III, had been soundly defeated by the rest of the rebel force. On the whole, however, the battles of the era were won by massed charges of knights, against which – it was thought – no force could stand.

Two more examples show the dominance of heavy cavalry in the thirteenth century, both of them victories of Charles of Anjou as he worked to establish himself as king of southern Italy and Sicily. Charles had been invited to rule this Kingdom of the Two Sicilies,

as it was known, the condition being that he had to defeat the Hohenstaufen, the pope's enemies, to establish his own rule. Charles brought a largely French force into his campaigns, buttressed by the promise of a crusading indulgence for their participation. In the Battle of Benevento on 26 February 1266, Charles had a very large cavalry force, numbering perhaps as much as 4600 men. His opponent, Manfred of Sicily, had fewer cavalrymen but a very large contingent of Muslim archers. Manfred, however, was willing to take the offensive, trusting in the strength of his mercenary German knights, who were apparently armed in advanced plate armour.

They were at a disadvantage since they had to cross a narrow bridge to engage the Angevins, relying on the protection of Manfred's archers as they did so. Charles' cavalry in a massed charge destroyed the Saracen archers, making it possible for the Angevins to surround the German knights and wear them down with successive charges launched against both flanks.

Although Manfred himself died on the field at Benevento, Charles had not yet won his crown. A final member of the Hohenstaufen dynasty, Conradin, rallied fresh opposition to the Angevin invasion. The resulting Battle of Tagliacozzo, fought on 23 August 1268, was a large-scale cavalry contest in which infantry played little part. Conradin's force won the initial advantage, fording the river and taking the Angevins on the flank. Once again, discipline and a commander with a clear overview of the battle were crucial. Conradin's knights thought they had won the day and chased the Angevins triumphantly from the field. But Charles had a hidden reserve, which he used to defeat the returning enemy cavalry as they straggled back on their tired horses.

WHEN CHARGES FAILED

Even in the golden days of the thirteenth century, the knightly charge was not a guarantee of success because so many factors were involved. But it is necessary to consider in greater detail a factor that rose to much greater visibility in the fourteenth century: the infantry. Battles ranging from Courtrai in 1302 to Agincourt in 1415 and beyond are hailed as great infantry victories, overcoming the glorious charges of knights

and replacing them with grubbier, bloodier and decidedly lower-class fighting techniques. Although it is true that dense infantry pike positions and careful massing of archers for the greatest effect became prominent in the fourteenth century, it is a caricature to imagine

Below: The Battle of Tagliacozzo (1268). Conradin escaped the rout of his army, but was soon captured and executed in the marketplace of Naples. He was only sixteen years old.

Above: The Battle of Legnano, at which the Lombard League defeated Frederick Barbarossa. Frederick eventually avenged what he saw as Henry the Proud's betrayal, seizing his duchies and exiling him from Germany.

Facing page: Emperor Frederick I Barbarossa (1152–90) honed his military skills with decades of campaigning in Italy. He led a vast army on the Third Crusade, but was drowned in Turkey.

that before that time infantry were practically unarmed, undisciplined, and of little use in a pitched battle.

Contemporary accounts – written by and for members of the knightly elite – often pass over the infantry, but there was no point in the Middle Ages at which infantry did not outnumber cavalry on the battlefield or at which well-marshalled foot soldiers did not

play a significant role. Even in the glory days of the knightly charge, cavalry forces could be defeated by their humbler brethren, often using the same weapons that are more famously associated with the infantry of the fourteenth century. Two great military engagements of the twelfth century – the Battle of Legnano and the Battle of Hattin – demonstrate effective infantry resistance even to the most determined attack.

Emperor Frederick Barbarossa fought for years to make good his claim to northern Italy, only to suffer a major defeat at the hands of the Lombard League on 29 May 1176 at the Battle of Legnano. Frederick's tactical skill could not save him from a fundamental problem: he did not have enough knights with him, because Duke Henry the Proud of Bavaria and

Saxony had refused his call for reinforcements. With the League's own heavy cavalry seriously outnumbering his own knights, the emperor seems to have counted on the nobility and valour of the cavalrymen he had to save the day (the Germans of this period often held Italian knights in contempt, especially as some were not of noble birth).

Frederick himself led a charge on the enemy's left wing, which consisted of infantrymen the Germans expected to drive apart in panic with relative ease. However, the Lombard wing held, not just because Frederick did not have enough knights but because these infantrymen were tougher than expected. A number of towns had provided trained militiamen armed with pikes, reinforcing their dense formations with dismounted

"The situation was different at the Battle of Hattin on 4 July 1187, Saladin's great victory over the assembled army of the Latin Kingdom of Jerusalem."

knights whose superior armour would allow them to meet any German knights who broke through on more equal terms. The Germans were indeed repulsed; Frederick himself was unhorsed and for a time believed to be dead, which began a panic among his own men. The Lombard cavalry then attacked Frederick's flank, completing their victory.

The situation was different at the Battle of Hattin on 4 July 1187, Saladin's great victory over the assembled army of the Latin Kingdom of Jerusalem. In this case, the Christian force included at least

Right: This illustration shows the Crusader foot soldiers making a last stand at Hattin as the lighter Muslim cavalry overwhelm them. This catastrophe led to the loss of Jerusalem.

1500 knights, which crusading experience had led them to expect was enough to take on any number of Muslim foes. As recently as the Battle of Mont-Gisard in 1177, the army of Jerusalem fighting under their king, Baldwin IV, had won a major victory over Saladin despite being badly outnumbered, Christian cavalry charges wreaking havoc among Saladin's surprised and disorganized troops.

In 1187, one of the largest armies ever assembled in the Crusader States marched to relieve the town of Tiberias, which Saladin was besieging. Although advised not to lead his force into a waterless district in mid-summer, King Guy appears to have been confident that he could get to a reliable water source and proceeded, thus playing into Saladin's hands. The Muslim army

Infantry Tactics Against The Charge

Above: Medieval infantrymen combined to see off cavalry attackers with a combination of pikes, spears and crossbow fire.

Pikes and arrows were the infantry weapons that, when used to the greatest tactical advantage, could stop the proudest knightly charge. But they had to be positioned and protected exactly right, and even then standing up to a charge of heavy cavalry remained a terrifying prospect. The issue was, above all, one of armour. Infantrymen by the fourteenth century were likely to wear some body armour; certainly they had helmets and shields and most often some protection for the torso. But commoner foot soldiers could not compete on anything like equal terms with knights, whose equipment by this time consisted of plate armour from head to toe. The quality of knights' armour all too often meant that they could just keep on coming no matter what means the enemy employed to try to stop them. The main weak point in their equipage was their horses; despite improvements in horse armour by the fourteenth century, it never completely covered the horse and knights who chose relative safety for their steeds had to sacrifice their mounts' speed and stamina. Massed archers could have a devastating effect on horses in a charge, but the archers had to be protected or the infuriated knights would ride right over them. The other option was tightly formed pikemen: horses would not charge into a solid formation, and then the pikes could be used against both horses and their riders.

> *"For the remaining knights, the only hope of survival was to break through – and break through quickly – to water. So they charged… repeatedly."*

Above: The Battle of Courtrai was a defeat that should not have happened. This illustration captures well the conditions the charging French knights had to face.

harried the Christians every step of the way, slowing their advance to a crawl to the point that they were forced to camp for the night before they reached water. By morning, the Jerusalemite army was in desperate straits, made even worse because Saladin's men lit grass fires so the smoke would blow over the thirsty Christians.

Most of the Christian infantry simply gave up, fleeing in small groups or surrendering in hope of some water. For the remaining knights, the only hope of survival was to break through – and break through quickly – to water. So they charged, and charged repeatedly. But it was impossible to dress a charge properly, with both mounts and men tormented by thirst and heavy Muslim archery fire further maddening the horses. The Christians' charge was held, all but

a contingent led by Raymond of Tripoli, which broke through to Lake Tiberias. The count made no effort to turn back and aid the rest of the cavalry force under King Guy, which made a further series of desperate charges in the hope of reaching and killing Saladin himself. Finally, the remnant of the crusader army surrendered.

THE THREAT OF PIKEMEN
The Battle of Courtrai, also known as the Battle of the Golden Spurs, exemplifies how well-trained pikemen could triumph over a knightly charge. Courtrai, fought on 11 July 1302 between a French royal army commanded by Robert of Artois and a coalition of Flemish rebels, can be characterized as a battle lost by the stupidity, or perhaps the overconfidence, of the commander. The Flemish

force consisted of urban militia infantry: uniformed men who had trained together. They were also well equipped, wearing mail and sometimes plate armour, carrying bows, crossbows, pikes and the infamous *goedendogs* – staffs 1.2–1.5m (4–5ft) long with a steel spike at the end. The Flemish took up a very strong defensive position; their flanks were protected by streams and the ground was marshy in front of them, an advantage they pushed further by digging trenches. Their intent was to slow or even halt the inevitable French cavalry charge. After all, Robert of Artois had 2500 heavy cavalrymen (both knights and men-at-arms) at his command, and a long-cultivated belief that French knights were the best in the world.

Robert gave a nod towards breaking down the solid Flemish ranks at the onset of the battle by loosing his crossbowmen against them. However, he seems to have been impatient to enter the action, so did not allow his own infantry time to do their work. Instead, the French cavalry forded the brook in front of the Flemings to begin the true assault. The conditions were horrendous for a charge. The Flemish line was quite close, so Robert's horsemen could not build up momentum, besides the problems of the ditches and marshy ground. Thus, as each wave of French knights reached the Flemish militiamen, their lines were ragged and they had little speed, giving the pikemen opportunities to stab the French horses and pull knights out of the saddle. The Flemings were not inclined to take prisoners in that desperate struggle. Robert of Artois

"The Flemish line was quite close, so Robert's horsemen could not build up momentum, besides the problems of the ditches and marshy ground."

Right: This fresco by Albrecht de Vriendt in the town hall of Bruges celebrates the Flemish victory over the French at the Battle of Courtrai.

himself was killed in the battle, along with all the other French commanders and between a third and a half of the French knights who took part in the battle. The Flemings hung the spurs of 500 of these knights in the church of St Mary, Courtrai, in thanksgiving for their victory.

Was Courtrai evidence that a new age of infantry had arrived, rendering the heavy cavalry

charge obsolete? It is doubtful that either side thought so. The Flemish position at Courtrai was particularly strong, and the French charges were particularly foolhardy under the circumstances. Moreover, the French eventually got their revenge, using conventional knightly charges to demolish armies of Flemish rebels at Cassel in 1328 and Roosebeke in 1382. Cassel was a particularly resounding victory: the Flemings started in a defensive position on a hill, but abandoned the advantage and attacked, making it possible for a series of charges commanded by King Philip VI to annihilate them.

Facing page: Edward III of England leading the English army across the Somme. Note the French pikemen on the far bank, doing nothing to impede the crossing.

CHARGES OF THE HUNDRED YEARS' WAR

Even though the Flemish victory over charging knights at Courtrai might be regarded as a fluke, it is hard to sustain that view when considering the great land battles of the Hundred Years' War. After all, in this great on-again/off-again conflict between England and France, the flower of French chivalry was brought

Below: This is the way a cavalry charge was supposed to work, the mounted knights destroying infantry formations, as in this painting of the Battle of Cassel (1328).

Left: French knights at Crécy charge the English longbow positions.

down no fewer than three times, and English longbowmen have received most of the credit. It is easy to oversimplify these great engagements – the battles of Crécy (1346), Poitiers (1356) and Agincourt (1415) – making the French sound old-fashioned or downright suicidal for sticking to outmoded knightly charges against a devastating storm of arrows. In reality, all three battles were hard-fought and the English were far from assured of victory in any. As in all battles, the factors that really counted were the quality of generalship and the morale of the men involved, even more than equipment or numbers.

In 1346, Edward III invaded France with a large army, emboldened by his naval victory at Sluys to lay claim to the French crown. The English army included about 2500 men-at-arms (this term is normally used by the fourteenth century to describe all heavy cavalry, whether they had been knighted or not), 3500 spearmen and 5000 longbowmen. The force that Philip VI of France brought against them had a significant number of crossbowmen (modern estimates range from 2000 to 6000), but vastly outnumbered the English in men-at-arms, perhaps as many as 12,000 of them.

As the battle approached on 25 August 1346, Philip moved his force in an effort to entrap and destroy the English. In response, King Edward did what good commanders had known to do for centuries: he carefully chose a defensible position near the village of Crécy and prepared to use it to the best possible advantage, positioning his men on a hill so any French charge would have to forge uphill, his flanks protected by natural features, ditches and pits dug in front. Archers were placed at the front, with the goal of further slowing any French charge, while Edward's men-at-arms were dismounted and placed to reinforce both the archers and the spearmen.

Such a deployment was vulnerable, but not to a cavalry charge, or at least not without desperate fighting. King Philip decided to attack as the contingents of his army reached Crécy, rather than allowing his men to rest for the night, further lessening their chance of success. But Philip does seem to have understood the danger of an immediate charge; he followed the usual military doctrine of the age by sending his mercenary crossbowmen forward first, expecting their bolts to disrupt the dense English formations and make a charge more likely to break through.

But crossbows are not well adapted to an advance under fire, being slow to load. In battle, crossbowmen normally fought in pairs, one man firing his weapon while the other provided shelter with an oversize shield (the *pavise*). Because Philip decided to engage immediately on arrival, his crossbowmen did not even have this defence, their *pavises* being still with the baggage. It is not surprising that the crossbowmen were soon repelled in some disorder.

"Their king ordered a charge against the still intact English lines, the French men-at-arms riding over their own retreating crossbowmen as they approached the English."

Above: The Battle of Poitiers, from Froissart's Chronicle. In reality, loosely formed and unprotected longbowmen would not have stood a chance against a cavalry charge.

Facing page: The capture of King John II at Poitiers, illustration by R.Caton (1894).

In the confusion of battle, the French suspected treachery. Their king ordered a charge against the still intact English lines, the French men-at-arms riding over their own retreating crossbowmen as they approached the English. This obstruction slowed the charge, as did the upward slope – and the thousands of English arrows launched against them. Even arrows shot from the most powerful longbow were unlikely to penetrate a plate armour breastplate, but they might pierce the lighter armour on limbs or a lucky shot could penetrate a visor. But horses, armoured lightly if at all, were not so lucky; the charge soon dissolved in a mass of wounded and dying horses and the men who became entangled with them.

The French charged again and again, making fifteen charges in all. One must ask why, since their first attempts were so unsuccessful. But Philip had his honour at stake, as well as his throne. French knights (including

King Philip) also had their pride, after over a century of dominating the battlefields of Europe. They must have thought that the English would eventually run out of arrows, rendering them easy prey for horsemen. In the event, the French nearly succeeded; one charge broke into the English vanguard, commanded by the Prince of Wales along with several more experienced officers. The Frenchmen of this charge soon discovered, though, that the archers were reinforced by men-at-arms, who were able to fight off the assault. As the sun set, about 1500 French men-at-arms lay dead on the field. King Edward

went on to take and fortify the city of Calais, to be used as a major staging ground for future campaigns in France.

To some extent, the French learned their lesson from Crécy and tried a different approach at the Battle of Poitiers on 19 September 1356. Again a French king was on the hunt, this time John II, who was attempting to cut off and destroy a much smaller English army commanded by Edward the Black Prince. Again the English had time to prepare a strong defensive position, the longbowmen who comprised nearly half of the force of 6000 men protected by hedges and stakes

and reinforced by men-at-arms. By comparison, the French king brought about 8000 men-at-arms to the field, but only about 3000 infantry, having made the decision to disband a very large infantry muster so that his army could move more quickly and cut the Black Prince off from retreat.

Although King John did not have infantry with missile weapons to soften the English lines before a charge, he proceeded with some caution, opening the engagement with a charge by a contingent of about 300 men-at-arms, apparently to test the strength of the English position. This first onslaught was easily repelled, their horses

"Prince Edward... remounted a contingent and sent them for a flank attack against the dismounted French, who, caught by surprise, were unable to respond..."

brought down by English arrows. The French king then decided to send his men-at-arms forward on foot, leaving their vulnerable horses in safety. The French men-at-arms were at a disadvantage: they had to march across a field and up a slope in their heavy plate armour and break past the English defences, all the while suffering a storm of arrows that would have wounded some and the force of which could knock a man off his feet at close range.

They *did* reach the English – at least some of them – and there was hard fighting along the line. What is usually forgotten about the Battle of Poitiers, however, is

Below: The crusaders' catastrophic defeat at the Battle of Nicopolis (1396) demonstrated the limits of the heavy cavalry charge.

Right: The payment of ransoms to Sultan Bayezid after the Battle of Nicopolis. The Ottomans executed many captives, saving only the wealthiest.

that it was a cavalry charge that decided the day, and that charge consisted of English men-at-arms. Most of Prince Edward's men-at-arms were dismounted to support his infantry, but when the battle was fully engaged, he remounted a contingent and sent them for a flank attack against the dismounted French, who, caught by surprise, were unable to respond and at a

serious disadvantage relative to their mounted opponents. An estimated 2500 Frenchmen died in the battle and a further 2000 were captured, including King John II. It is interesting to note that at the Battle of Agincourt in 1415 the French did not even attempt a mounted charge.

THE END OF THE CHARGE?

The Western European battles of the fourteenth century demonstrated the vulnerability of the knightly charge – as long as the conditions were exactly right

for defence. Courtrai, Crécy and Poitiers could all have gone the other way, if only the men-at-arms in the initial charge had found a single point at which they could break through the enemy line. Two final battles, both involving charges that ultimately failed, help drive home the lesson that the heavy cavalry charge still had an important role to play, as long as the cavalry was well handled.

The Battle of Nicopolis, fought on 25 September 1396, was an extraordinary battle, at which a Christian crusading force

Above: English troops, broken by a French cavalry charge, are cut down as they flee. From a fifteenth-century illuminated copy of Froissart's Chronicle.

dominated by French men-at-arms went down in a devastating defeat to the Ottoman Turks. By this time, Europeans were alarmed at the Ottoman advance into Europe, and a new wave of crusade fervour had created a large army that included both crusaders and the royal and princely armies of several Eastern European states. The force was plagued by internal dissension about goals and tactics. Sultan Bayezid, by contrast, marshalled his force well, which proved to be the crusaders' undoing.

At Nicopolis, the French cavalry demanded the honour of the first attack, although they were advised not to do so. But they soon discovered that a series of traps had been created for them. All the French knights would have been able to see as they launched their charge was Muslim light cavalry, and they would have known from tales of their crusading ancestors that such fighters could not stand up to Western chivalry. The French soon broke through the enemy line, only to discover that the light cavalrymen had been positioned as a screen for what lay ahead. The French reached a belt of sharpened stakes, filled with Turkish archers. Soon most of the French horses were killed or wounded. However, rather than withdrawing, the French men-at-arms continued forward on foot (one chronicler tells that, anticipating this need, the French knights cut off the long points of their shoes before leaving

camp). They climbed uphill to the enemy, uprooted the stakes, and routed the bowmen. Then, as they reached the top of the hill in exhausted triumph, they found a third Turkish force, Bayezid's fresh heavy cavalry, waiting for them. Most of the crusader army was annihilated or captured.

Nicopolis is a testament to the ongoing effectiveness of cavalry charges. If all that the French men-at-arms had faced had been the Muslim light infantry, it would have been a Christian triumph. It also testifies to the sheer tenacity and fighting ability of French chivalry, since the men in the advance successfully transitioned to fighting on foot and overwhelmed a heavily defended enemy position.

Above all, though, Nicopolis teaches a lesson about the need for careful intelligence work. The Western knights do not seem to have been aware of the fighting capabilities of the Ottoman heavy cavalry, although their Eastern European allies tried to warn them. And Bayezid had prepared the trap cleverly, drawing the crusaders in while hiding his heavy cavalrymen on the reverse side of a slope.

> " *The Western knights do not seem to have been aware of the fighting capabilities of the Ottoman heavy cavalry, although their Eastern European allies tried to warn them.*"

BATTLE OF VERNEUIL

To return to Western Europe, a final example from later in the Hundred Years' War demonstrates that the effectiveness of the knightly charge was not yet over. This was the Battle of Verneuil (17 August 1424), a major engagement fought between the English commanded by John, Duke of Bedford, and a French force supported by Scottish archers. As had become the English habit in their wars with France, Duke John assumed a defensive position when the superior French force arrived on the scene, but his plan nearly went disastrously wrong. The English archers were, as usual, placed forward where their shots could be effective, their line reinforced with men-at-arms and protected by stakes driven into the ground in front of them. But the summer had been hot and the ground baked hard, so the stakes could not be dug in deeply. The French opened the engagement with

a massed cavalry charge: 2000 Lombard mercenaries, clad in the latest steel plate armour. Although they must have suffered injuries to their horses, the Lombards broke through, sweeping aside the stakes and crashing into the English line

with enough force to create chaos. They penetrated the line completely, many Englishmen fleeing in panic (one captain was later drawn and quartered for his cowardice in withdrawing the 500 men under his command, thinking the battle lost).

At Verneuil, the Lombard charge was effective, but the Lombard men-at-arms failed to follow up their triumph. Instead, they went on to attack the English baggage train, leaving their French comrades to deal with the brunt of battle. The Duke of Bedford successfully rallied his troops and proved triumphant in a bloody and drawn-out hand-to-hand engagement, the Lombards returning to the battlefield to find the battle lost. As had been the case for centuries, a charge could still be effective. But at Verneuil, as for many battles in the past, the decisive factor was not the charge itself but whether the successful cavalrymen followed up on their triumph.

Left: Notorious as the man who ordered the execution of Joan of Arc, Henry V's brother John of Bedford ably fought to complete the conquest of France for his nephew Henry VI.

Knightly Orders

When the armies of the First Crusade took Jerusalem on 15 July 1099, few of the participants would have been so naïve as to believe their task was complete. Indeed, within a few days they had to march out of Jerusalem to meet and defeat a large Fatimid army that had come to the relief of Jerusalem. But after their final victory at Ascalon on 12 August, many crusaders returned to Europe, having fulfilled their vows and won eternal glory for themselves and their families.

By one estimate, only 200 Western knights and 700 infantrymen remained in the newly established kingdom of Jerusalem. Around them was a roiling sea of enemies, eager to retake the territory the crusaders had seized if opportunity presented itself. Godfrey of Bouillon, the newly elected Christian ruler of Jerusalem, would have known full well that his new kingdom was little more than a single city, with limited access to the sea and very little of the surrounding territory. It was not a viable state, and expansion was essential for survival. He might not have realized at first, though, what difficulties bands of raiding Muslims would cause, both to his own new subjects and to the tens of thousands of pilgrims who began flocking to the holy places.

THE FOUNDING OF THE KNIGHTS TEMPLARS

Protection for pilgrims, who by long-standing tradition did not themselves bear arms, was a central problem in the first years of the Latin Kingdom of Jerusalem. Pilgrims were eager not just to visit Jerusalem, but also the other locales associated with the life of Christ. Bethlehem was in Latin hands, but the road there was dangerous. Even more perilous was the route through the desert to the River Jordan, where pilgrims went to pray and bathe in memory of Jesus' baptism. In a particularly notorious incident, just before Easter in 1119 Muslim raiders killed 300 pilgrims going to the Jordan, and captured 60 more. This event was probably the catalyst for the first military religious order, an organization of knights vowed to permanent service of Christianity.

A French knight named Hugh de Payens lived in the kingdom of Jerusalem, apparently remaining there after accompanying his lord on one of the small crusading expeditions that provided regular reinforcements for the struggling kingdom. He and eight companions – all of whom were his relatives by blood or marriage – formed a confraternity, a voluntary association to provide military escorts for pilgrims. But unlike any other confraternity, they took things a step further by taking permanent vows, pledging themselves to lives of service that would be lived in a state of

Facing page: The crusader assault on Jerusalem in 1099 was a desperate struggle for a great goal: this illustration depicts Christ's passion on the walls above the attacking crusaders.

Right: The seal of the Knights Templars – two knights on a single horse – is emblematic of their vows of poverty and brotherhood.

First Seal of the Knights Templars.

personal poverty, chastity, and obedience to their superior. As a symbol of their humble service, they adopted as their seal the image of two knights riding on a single horse – although of course knights could not fight effectively that way. King Baldwin II of Jerusalem, perennially short of manpower, gave his approval to the new organization as well as part of his palace for the nine knights to live. Since the royal palace was in the al-Aqsa Mosque, which westerners believed to be the Temple of Solomon, the little military force came to be known as Knights of the Temple of Solomon, or simply the Knights Templar.

In 1126, Hugh de Payens returned to Europe to recruit additional manpower, since his organization still had only nine members. He went to his native region of Champagne, and to further his efforts he appeared before the Council of Troyes in 1128. The Templars were a startling innovation in the world of professed religious life. Christian authorities had always been very ambivalent towards fighting and bloodshed, and when men became monks by definition this meant giving up arms and the warrior's life. As we have seen, however, knights themselves had other ideas of religious dedication, crafting by this period a uniquely chivalric brand of piety that glorified warfare as long as it was conducted for a worthy cause. Thus, although the notion of

"Bernard... saw the potential of this new military order, both for defence of the Holy Land and to save the souls of knights, so he gave Hugh and his companions his wholehearted support."

fighting monks was outlandish, it was no longer completely repugnant, and the assembled bishops and abbots at Troyes approved this new order of Knights Templar.

BERNARD OF CLAIRVAUX
Among the churchmen who met at Troyes was Bernard, the abbot of Clairvaux. Bernard was the son of a knightly family who had only entered monastic life as an adult. He saw the potential of this new military order, both for defence of the Holy Land and to save the souls of knights, so he gave Hugh and his companions his wholehearted support. And Bernard's support was well worth having. Widely recognized as a saint in his own lifetime, his enormous influence led to a massive expansion of his own

Above: Pope Honorius II officially recognized the Templars as a religious order in 1128, as shown here in François Granet's 1840 painting.

Right: Templars wore a distinctive white mantle marked with a red cross; although attention focuses on the knights of the order, there were also priests, non-noble fighters and support staff.

Facing page: Alfonso I 'the Battler' of Aragon was one of the first to see the value of the military orders in providing a defence against the Muslims.

"Bernard bitterly mocks and reproaches the secular knights of his day, characterizing them as frivolous wastrels who … pass their time in gaming, hunting and storytelling."

monastic order, the Cistercians. His preaching later brought the Second Crusade into being. Now, however, he preached the glories of a new, purified knighthood, dedicated to defence of fellow Christians and the holy places. The most famous of Bernard's effort to popularize the Templars is a treatise, *In Praise of the New Knighthood*, which he wrote in the early 1130s at Hugh de Payens' request.

The message of *In Praise of the New Knighthood* is simple: Knights, says Bernard, should save their souls by joining this great new cause. Bernard bitterly mocks and reproaches the secular knights of his day, characterizing them as frivolous wastrels who bedeck themselves like women and pass their time in gaming, hunting and storytelling. Instead of living a life mired in sin, they should be *true* knights, dedicating themselves to God in defence of the Holy Land.

Bernard's call resonated with the knights of Europe. Recruits began flocking to the Templars. Some joined the order only for a term, such as Count Henry of Champagne, who spent a campaigning season in Jerusalem in confraternity with the Templars. Non-knights also joined the young order as sergeants, as priests or as lay brothers. At the heart of the order, however, stood the knights, who soon numbered in their hundreds.

Thousands more were eager to support the cause but could not join the order because of age, infirmity or other commitments. They could support the Templars, however, with their donations. It was expensive to equip an effective fighting force in the Crusader States. Arms and armour had to be purchased and maintained, and horses needed constant replacement. The Templars had to feed themselves and also feed and equip the large numbers of mercenaries they hired as well as crusaders who fought alongside the order for a time. Soon they were also entrusted with castles along the frontier of the Latin Kingdom, many of which were built at their own expense, adding another massive cost.

Recognition of these needs led to the creation of a vast international supply network. Men and women in Europe would make gifts to the Templars, often in their wills – sometimes the donation would be cash, but often a dying knight would bequeath his armour or a horse to the order. Many others would donate land, which would generate a permanent income, but had to be overseen and the profits somehow funnelled across the Mediterranean to where they were needed for the ongoing work of defence. These gifts varied enormously in size, from the toll of a single bridge to the great bequest of King Alfonso I of Aragon, who in 1134 tried to leave his entire kingdom to the Templars, the Hospitallers and the canons of the Holy Sepulchre. Although Alfonso's testament was overturned, the Templars still acquired important estates in Aragon.

Within decades, a complex system to maintain estates and remit profits had developed, both for the Templars and for other orders. In the case of the Templars, estates and other resources would be consolidated as much as possible with exchanges and sometimes purchases, and each cluster of landed resources would be placed under the authority of a local commander, a man who was frequently a knight too old for military service. The work of the local commandery was twofold: to send money and other supplies east and to recruit new members for the order. In the process, the Templars developed a complex banking system, which they made available to crusaders, who, for example, could deposit their crusading war chest in Paris and then draw on it with letters of credit in Jerusalem. The first record of Templar banking comes from as early as 1135.

"The development of Krak des Chevaliers was a feat of castle-building comparable to the fortress the Templars created at Gaza..."

Left: An artist's impression of Raymond du Puy, who transformed the Hospitallers into a military order. Shown here in the distinctive black habit with white cross of the order.

Above: Krak des Chevaliers, the greatest fortress of the Kingdom of Jerusalem, was held by the Hospitallers until it fell to Mamluk attack in 1271.

KNIGHTS HOSPITALLER TRANSFORMED

Although the origins of the Knights Templar are clear, the same cannot be said of their chief rival order in the Holy Land, the Knights of the Hospital of St John of Jerusalem. As their name implies, the Hospitallers started as a conventional, peaceful order dedicated to nursing and providing hospitality for pilgrims to the holy places. They operated a hospital (which included the functions of a hospice as well as service to the sick and wounded) in Jerusalem by 1080. When the Crusader States were established with the success of the First Crusade, their first prior, a man named Gerard, seized the opportunity to establish new hospitals for pilgrims and crusaders. This enlarged nursing order received papal recognition in 1113. These first Hospitallers' association with pilgrims probably explains how they came to militarize; it is likely

that they began to support fighting men to protect their own holdings and pilgrims before they began admitting active fighting men to the order.

It was probably in the 1120s that the Hospital of St John of Jerusalem began to profess knights as members, continuing to employ them in a military role in the fashion of the Templars. Grand Master Raymond du Puy (1120–60) built up an effective military force, although not neglecting the order's original nursing mission. He put this force at the disposal of King Fulk of Jerusalem, who in 1136 granted the Hospitallers the town of Bethgibelin on the frontier to defend.

Like the Templars, the Hospitallers' permanent vows provided a stability that waves of crusaders who came for a single campaign and then left could not. Their very permanence – and the support of European donations – made both Hospitallers and Templars ideal frontier troops. Bethgibelin was the first of many such gifts to the Hospitallers, if such an expensive responsibility can be regarded as a gift. The other rulers of the Crusader States soon emulated King Fulk. In 1144, the Count of Tripoli granted the Hospitallers a series of castles and two towns on his frontier, with the vital mission of protecting his territory against the onslaughts

of the belligerent Zengi, Muslim ruler of Mosul and Aleppo. One of the towns was Krak, which came to be known as Krak des Chevaliers ('of the Knights'). The Hospitallers developed the castle of Krak massively and provided it with a strong garrison, all at their own expense. The development of Krak des Chevaliers was a feat of castle-building comparable to the fortress the Templars created at Gaza after they were granted control of it in c. 1150.

OTHER HOLY LAND ORDERS

Other Holy Land military religious orders emerged about the same time as the Templars and Hospitallers, although none

Above: Knights of the Orders of Calatrava and Aviz. As these eighteenth-century illustrations show, the Spanish military orders continued in existence long after the end of the Reconquest.

rose to such great prominence. An interesting example is the Order of St Lazarus, established in c. 1123. Like the Hospitallers, at first the Lazarites were a nursing order, dedicated to the care of lepers. At some point the leprous knights in their care began conducting military missions. Indeed, the Templars ordered that if any of their own brethren contracted the disease they must transfer to the Knights of St Lazarus, where they could continue to fight until they were too incapacitated.

A similar process took place on the Iberian Peninsula, where the small Christian kingdoms of the north began the long process of winning back territory from the Muslims (the *Reconquista*) in the eleventh century. This was the second great crusading front, popes offering crusading indulgences to fighters who went to Spain to join in the holy war. In the 1120s – at the same time that the Templars and Hospitallers emerged as military orders in the Holy Land – Spain saw the foundation of confraternities of knights to serve the cause of reconquest. These confraternities were sworn associations of warriors dedicated to the war against Islam, and proved to be focal points for men

who wanted to participate in campaigns. From there it was but a short step to military religious orders whose members took permanent vows.

The earliest military order on the Iberian Peninsula was the Order of Calatrava and, as in the Crusader States, the starting point was the desperate need for defence along the Muslim–Christian frontier. Alfonso VII of León and Castile took the Muslim-held town of Calatrava in 1147. Having no fighting men to spare, the king turned it over to the Templars to defend. But the Templars' focus was on the Holy Land, not Spain, especially as this was the period of the Second Crusade, when the Templars strongly supported

"The Knights of Santiago maintained a hospitaller role as well as fighting, and were unique among the military religious orders in accepting married brethren."

Right: A Knight of Santiago, wearing the order's flowing robes marked with a dagger-shaped red cross.

King Louis VII of France. So they soon abandoned their new charge in Spain, leaving a group of Cistercian monks to step in and assume Calatrava's defence. It is not clear if those first Cistercians actually bore arms or perhaps financed knights to do the fighting instead, but soon the community of Calatrava began admitting knights to play a military function in the nascent order, which won formal recognition in 1164. The Calatravans prospered, especially after 1173, when Alfonso VIII granted the order one-fifth of all land taken from the Muslims.

Other orders flourished in Spain. One of the earliest was the Portuguese Order of Aviz, which was organized in c. 1146 and played a significant role at least from 1166, when Alfonso, the first King of Portugal, gave them the town of Évora to defend. They soon moved their headquarters to the major castle of Aviz. Similarly, the Order of Alcántara was established on the frontier of León by 1170 and received papal recognition in 1176. The year before, the pope had also recognized the Order of Santiago. This order had its start protecting and caring for pilgrims to the

shrine of St James (Santiago) in Compostella. The Knights of Santiago maintained a hospitaller role as well as fighting, and were unique among the military religious orders in accepting married brethren.

DEFENCE OF THE HOLY LAND

Wherever they operated, the military religious orders could offer disciplined, experienced knights to provide leadership and a vital striking force in war, as well as sergeants and hired infantrymen and light cavalry. The Crusader States especially, with their relatively small numbers of permanent settlers of knightly rank, reinforced by irregular waves of crusaders, could not long have survived without the orders, knights repeatedly proving their ability to defeat superior numbers of more lightly armed Muslim fighters. Over time, the orders appear to have taken rather too much pride in their expertise, winning resentment and dislike in the process, even while their military abilities were acknowledged to be essential.

Bands of pilgrims and crusaders would often join in temporary confraternity with a military order while they were in the Holy Land, receiving in return protection and a chance to fight with the knights. But to fight alongside the Templars or Hospitallers meant accepting their discipline. One can see a taste of this on the Second Crusade, after Louis VII of France's army suffered near disaster. Louis, unable to control his own knights, put Templar officers in charge of the army's march. The Templars imposed discipline, including forcing the crusaders to suffer attacks without responding and instead only to attack on command, and to return to the army when the retreat was sounded. They welded the struggling French army into a force where knights could fight effectively.

Right: The departure of the French army under King Louis VII on the Second Crusade in 1147, a fresco from Cressac-sur-Charente, France.

The fighting members of the orders spent years or decades in the east, acquiring local knowledge that was invaluable but sometimes provoked outrage in newcomers. For example, military orders sometimes imposed tribute on neighbouring enemy territory, instead of existing in a state of constant war. The Muslim chronicler Usama ibn Munqidh even tells of how the Templars protected a Muslim pilgrim to Jerusalem from the harassment of a

Western crusader who protested at the Muslim turning towards Mecca to pray.

The papacy acknowledged how vital the military orders were to the defence of the holy places. The popes gave their formal approval to the orders – for example, the Templars in 1139 with the bull *Omne datum optimum* ('Every perfect gift'). This bull placed the young order under papal protection, exempting it from the authority of local bishops. Christians were encouraged to make donations to the order with another papal bull of 1144, while a third bull in 1145 gave the Templars an extraordinary variety of special rights and privileges, including the authority to build

their own churches and operate their own cemeteries, both of which encroached on the rights of local clergy.

RESENT OF THE ORDERS

Resentment of the orders' special rights, which stripped needed money from the struggling bishoprics of the Crusader States, sometimes boiled over into violence. The patriarchs of both Jerusalem and Antioch appealed to Rome, hoping in vain that the pope would rein in the orders. The knights responded vigorously – one should remember that these were members of the elite military class, trained from childhood not to flinch from conflict. Indeed, when the patriarch of Jerusalem complained about the Hospitallers in 1154, they reacted by attacking the Church of the Holy Sepulchre, even firing arrows into that holiest of buildings. In 1179, the Third Lateran Council demanded that the military orders behave better, finally responding to complaints about their arrogance and greed, but the council's demand seems to have made little difference.

The simple truth was that the orders operated, for better or worse, by the knightly ideals of their age. They were also essential, and their leaders knew as much. By 1187, the Hospitallers, for example, held twenty important castles in the Crusader States. Moreover, they provided at least as much manpower to the armies of the Latin Kingdom as did secular knights. Kings had to ask for their service for campaigns rather than demanding it as a right, but it was rare for the orders to refuse to support any attack on the Muslim enemy. This could lead to conflict within the ranks.

A notorious example is the siege of Ascalon in 1153. The Templars with the army breached the wall, breaking their way into the town. A contemporary account tells that the Templars then refused to let non-Templars join the fray, wanting all the glory (and booty) for themselves. It is also quite possible that the secular knights refused to follow the Templars into the breach. Whichever the case, the result was a disaster. Without support and reinforcements, the forty Templars who had broken into Ascalon were all killed, their

Below: The castle of Kerak in Jordan is a typical fortress of the Crusader States. It surrendered to Saladin in 1188 in the aftermath of the Battle of Hattin.

Above: The siege of Ascalon (1153). The fifteenth-century artist has given the Christian army the weapons of his own time, but accurately depicts the ongoing struggle to secure the territory of Jerusalem.

bodies hung from the battlements by the mocking defenders.

More frequently, however, the order personnel and secular knights appear to have worked together amicably. In the Battle of Mount Gisard (1177), for instance, the Templars accepted orders from King Baldwin IV, who, despite his growing debility from leprosy, soundly defeated a Muslim invasion army with the small force of Templars and secular knights at his disposal.

By the 1170s, the Templars maintained a force of about 600 knights and 2000 sergeants in the east; the Hospitallers were only slightly smaller. They provided at least half of the regular fighting force – both knights and hired infantry and light cavalry – of the kings of Jerusalem, as well as supporting the prince of Antioch and the count of Tripoli. The Muslim forces arrayed against them never developed a reliable means to combat these heavily armed, well-disciplined professional fighting men. And Muslim princes recognized that the knights of the orders were their most formidable enemies.

THE THIRD CRUSADE AND THE NEW ORDERS

The executions after Hattin, although a heavy blow, were soon recouped as the Templars and Hospitallers called for reinforcements from their European commanderies and

"Besides bringing new Hospitallers and Templars to the east, though, the Third Crusade also saw the creation of two new military religious orders…"

A Battle With Thirst

Sultan Saladin invaded the Kingdom of Jerusalem in the summer of 1187, launching his attack against the town of Tiberias. King Guy of Jerusalem took the bait, marching his army through waterless territory in the summer heat, slowed by constant harassment from Saladin's troops. The army, which included about 1200 knights, half of them members of the orders, was forced to camp before reaching water, and the Muslims made their plight even more desperate by lighting grass fires, exacerbating the Christians' thirst with the smoke.

Most of the Christian infantry broke and fled even before battle was engaged on 4 July, leaving the knights without their vital support. The result was Saladin's greatest victory; at the end of the day almost the entire Christian army had been killed or captured.

In the aftermath of the battle, Saladin purchased the Templars and Hospitallers who had survived the engagement from their captives, then had them beheaded. The only exception was the master of the Temple, Gerard de Ridefort, who was released in return for surrendering the great Templar fortress of Gaza.

Right: Gustave Doré presents Saladin as a triumphant, heroic figure in this nineteenth-century engraving.

recruited new members. By the time of the Battle of Arsuf in 1191, there were sufficient Hospitallers in the Holy Land for Richard the Lionheart, the dominant leader of the Third Crusade, to commit the rearguard of his march to their protection.

Besides bringing new Hospitallers and Templars to the east, though, the Third Crusade also saw the creation of two new military religious orders, designed to satisfy the needs of pious knights from other parts of Europe than the dominantly French orders already active in the Holy Land. The two new orders, the Knights of St Thomas Acon and the Order of Brothers of the German House of St Mary in Jerusalem (more familiarly known as the Teutonic Knights), both emerged in the hideous conditions of the siege of Acre. After he was released after the Battle of Hattin, King Guy of Jerusalem began besieging Acre with the small force at his command. As crusaders arrived, answering the pope's urgent cry for help from the knights of the West to regain Jerusalem, they attached themselves to the siege, suffering much from enemy attacks and disease. Organizing to help the crusaders from their own region characterized both of these new foundations.

The first, the Knights of St Thomas of Canterbury at Acre (usually Anglicized to 'Acon'), was an English order. Englishmen had begun arriving in the east long

Below: The Battle of Arsuf defeated but failed to destroy Saladin's army. Here, Richard the Lionheart is shown leading the charge.

Facing page: Christian forces, especially
members of the military orders, fought
desperately to keep Acre in 1291, the
last port remaining to serve future
crusaders. Only when all was lost did
some of the defenders save themselves
by ship.

Right: Hermann von Salza's leadership
of the Teutonic Knights was crucial to
the success of the order and he is still
celebrated today.

before their king arrived, and
many soon found themselves in
need. Thus a group of men banded
together as a hospitaller order in
1191. At first the Knights of St
Thomas were non-military, but
once again the ongoing needs of
the Christians in the east led to an
order's militarization, in this case
at the time of the Fifth Crusade
(1217–21). They were never a
large order and, unique among the
military religious orders, voluntarily
abandoned their military role again
after the final Mamluk conquest of
the Crusader States.

By contrast, the Teutonic
Knights came to play a highly
visible and significant role in
history. Like the Knights of St
Thomas, they started at the siege of
Acre by providing care particularly
for German crusaders. Indeed,
the Germans who made it to Acre
needed all the help they could
get. The enormous army that had
set out under Emperor Frederick
Barbarossa had dissolved into
chaos after Frederick drowned
in a river in Turkey. Only about
5000 men – discouraged and
disorganized – made it to Acre.
The first Teutonic Knights
struggled mightily to help their
fellow Germans, impressing Duke

Frederick of Swabia so much that
he wrote to his brother, the new
emperor Henry VI, asking for
imperial support for the new order.

The Teutonic Knights
militarized only a few years later,
to support Henry VI's crusade
in 1197. After that, their rise to
prominence was rapid as they
gained recruits and donations,
mostly from the German lands.
The master of the order from about
1209 on, Hermann von Salza,
played a major role in that rise.
He proved very helpful to German
crusaders during the Fifth Crusade,
in the process winning himself a
place in all major councils. The
order was showered with gifts in
the wake of the crusade. By 1230,
the Teutonic Knights had about
26 hospitals in the east, as well as
a military organization that was
regarded as equal to that of the
Hospitallers and Templars.

HERMANN VON SALZA

No order was shaped so much
by an individual as the Teutonic
Knights were by Hermann von
Salza, the son of a minor knightly
family who rose from the ranks
to lead the fledgling order. Much
of Hermann's success was due
to his staunch support of the
German emperor Frederick II.
Most of Frederick's reign was
embroiled in conflict with the
papacy. Frederick vowed to go
on crusade but then delayed, so
the pope excommunicated him.
Frederick then went on crusade
anyway in 1228, despite papal
fulminations, and the Teutonic
Order supported him, despite the
fact that it meant co-operating
with an excommunicate. In
reality, Hermann had little choice,
because most of his order's lands
lay in imperial territory, but the
pope responded by revoking the

Teutonic order's independence and placing them under the command of the Hospitallers. Hermann soon won forgiveness and renewed rights for his order, while remaining on good terms with the emperor. This served his order in good stead, as the Teutonic Knights gradually shifted their focus from the Holy Land to the eastern frontiers of Europe.

Very early in Hermann von Salza's mastership, in 1211, King Andrew II of Hungary had asked for the Teutonic Knights' help against the nomadic Cumans, giving the knights land in Transylvania as a buffer to protect Hungarian lands from the Cuman raids. The Teutonic Knights established themselves in Burzenland rapidly, building at

least five castles even while they remained heavily engaged in the ongoing effort to win Jerusalem back from the Muslims. But King Andrew soon began to regret his invitation, as the Teutonic Knights, who answered to the pope rather than any local king, began to assert their independence and encroach on neighbouring Hungarian nobles. In 1225,

Above: Although in ruins, the castle of Cesis in Latvia bears testimony to the strength of the Teutonic Order in the region.

Facing page: In the Fifth Crusade (1217–1221), the western forces were held together by a papal legate, Cardinal Pelagius. Here he is depicted preparing to disembark at Damietta, Egypt.

Andrew made the decision to expel the order from the territory they had been given, despite papal efforts to protect them.

The very next year, however, Duke Conrad of Masovia invited the Teutonic Knights to play a similar role in his own border region of Kulm. This time, Hermann von Salza insisted on greater security in form of an imperial confirmation that they would be sovereign over the land they gained, which he received with the Golden Bull of Rimini (so-called because it was sealed with a gold seal instead of the usual wax) in 1226. At first, the knights could not move into Kulm; they were occupied in the east, first with the end of the Fifth Crusade and then with Frederick II's expedition. Losing patience, Duke Conrad founded his own order in 1228 to provide some protection for the border, the Knights of Dobrin, but that organization remained small. Starting in 1230, though, the Teutonic Knights began to focus on the Baltic and eventually the Knights of Dobrin amalgamated with them.

THE FORTUNES OF THE TEUTONIC ORDER

Fighting was fierce in the Baltic. The Prussians were still polytheists, as were the Lithuanians, Livonians and Estonians beyond them, and the frontier with the Christian lands was plagued with frequent raids. The newly named bishop of Riga had founded his own military order in c. 1202, the Swordbrethren, to help protect and expand Christian control in Livonia. The short history of this Order of the Sword was plagued by conflict with their own bishop, by lack of discipline, and by their serious defeat at the hands of the Kurs in 1237. After being defeated, the surviving Swordbrethren joined the Teutonic Knights.

Even with this reinforcement, the Teutonic Order was badly overextended in the 1240s and 1250s, struggling to maintain a military force in both the Holy Land and the Baltic. The order split into factions over which region to prioritize. Their foes were particularly numerous and powerful on both fronts in those years, and the knights suffered major losses in a number of battles. In 1241, the Prussian master of the order joined a

Right: An army made up of Poles and Moravians with support from the Teutonic Knights tried and failed to stop the Mongol invasion of Europe at Liegnitz in 1241.

Facing page: The Battle on the Ice (1242) was a great victory for Alexander Nevsky of Novgorod, and a humiliating defeat for the Teutonic Knights.

northern army to combat the Mongols, only to be soundly defeated in the Battle of Liegnitz.

The very next year, the order's army was bested again when fighting Alexander Nevsky of Novgorod in the Battle of Lake Peipus, also known as the Battle on the Ice because it was fought on the frozen lake. Lake Peipus demonstrates clearly the Teutonic Order's territorial ambitions. The order had invaded Novgorod – a Christian principality – attempting to take advantage of the confusion the Mongols had brought to the region.

For the most part, however, the Teutonic Knights fought non-Christians in the Baltic, and the war in Prussia gradually became the order's main focus, although they continued to maintain a presence in the east until the final fall of Acre in 1291. For fifty years they waged a bitter war to subdue the Prussians, then turned to the pagan Lithuanians (whose territory lay between the Order's holdings in Prussia and those in Livonia they had gained with the incorporation of the Swordbrethren). They were aided in their efforts by a constant flow of Western knights, eager to show their mettle against a worthy foe and to win a crusading indulgence in the process.

> *"In 1241, the Prussian master of the order joined a northern army to combat the Mongols, only to be soundly defeated in the Battle of Liegnitz."*

LIFE IN THE ORDERS

The knights who joined one of the military religious orders lived highly structured lives. They took permanently binding vows of poverty, chastity and obedience, and lived by a rule like that of monks (although allowed to eat meat because of their strenuous military duties). Most accounts focus on their military discipline, but their religious duties were also strenuous – for example, Templars were ordered to repeat the Lord's Prayer sixty times every morning. They could be given humiliating

КНЗЬ АЛЕЗАНРА . МНОГОХРАБРЫ . ГАКОДРЕВЛЕ Оу
Оумралоа . СЛНІКРТПЦІН . ГАПШОВАЛЕ ЛНКАГО
КНЗЬ АЛЕЗАНРА . НЕПОЛНИШАДА РАТНАГО . БАХУ БО
СРДАНАКНПО . ГАКОШЛООГНЖЕНАШЬ ЧТНЫ . НДРА
ГІН . НПКВПРНЕПТКОРЕМА . ПОЛОЖНГЛАВЫСВОА ЗАТА .
ВЕГІНЖЕ СНААЛЕЗАНРТ . ПВЗДВРОУЦКВОННАНБО
НРЕ . СОДНЖЕНРАССОДИПРЮМОЮ . ГЛАЗЫКАПЕЛЕ
РОВЧНЦАПОМОБ НГН . ГАКОДРЕВЛЕМОНПТВЕНННААМА
ЛНКА . НПРАДЕ ДУ МОЕМ У КНЗЮ ГАРОСЛАВУ . НА ОКА
ЖННАГОГПОПОЛКА :-

The Grand Tour For Knights

Campaigning with the Teutonic Knights became for over a century the medieval equivalent of the grand tour for young men of noble family. The knights organized two campaigns a year, one in the summer and one in the winter (when they could take advantage of the frozen ground for greater mobility). The order's officials would entertain their crusading visitors in style, then would use them to supplement the order's forces to attack a particular objective, most often a border fortress. The guests would have the thrill of real war for the sake of Christ, but with limited danger (although there are tales of angry Prussians roasting knights in full armour over slow fires). The most famous of these crusaders to the Teutonic Order State was Henry of Bolingbroke, who later became King Henry IV of England. In 1390–1, he took a party of 32 knights and squires to the Baltic to fight with the Teutonic Knights for a season.

Right: Before he became king, the future Henry IV of England won military glory by campaigning with the Teutonic Order.

penances for infractions, such as being ordered to eat their meals seated on the floor of the hall rather than with their fellow knights. For failure to obey orders on the battlefield they could be beaten or, in extreme cases, expelled from the order. A higher level of discipline was expected of these monk-knights than of their secular brethren, and the knights of the orders usually lived up to expectations.

Why, then, for centuries did young men of good family join the military religious orders? The knightly orders were a good career option for landless younger sons – certainly more secure than joining the household of a lord and hoping to win rewards through outstanding service. Becoming a soldier of Christ in this way was also more agreeable to someone raised as a knight than the other

career track for younger sons, the way of traditional monasticism or the priesthood. They were assured of good equipment and horses, faithful comrades and honoured care in sickness and old age. The upper officers of the orders usually came from higher social ranks than the ordinary knights (although Hermann von Salza of the Teutonic Knights was of insignificant birth), but there was considerable room to rise by merit. Nor were even simple knights mere followers with no say in their fate. All the military orders had periodic chapter meetings, at which senior brethren met to make important decisions for the order.

It is also important to remember that the chivalric ideals in which knights were immersed from childhood included a very strong element of Christian piety, including the constantly repeated refrain that there was no higher calling than to fight for God, which inspired hundreds of thousands to take crusading vows. To give oneself over to God suited medieval ideas of penance. Indeed, men sometimes joined one of the military orders on their deathbeds – for example, William Marshal or the crusader state baron John of Ibelin. For those in good health, though, to join an order was essentially to become a permanent crusader, and assuredly such men expected a reward in heaven.

A recent analysis of Templar records has shown that knights usually joined the order when they were in their twenties, after they had already gained some years of military experience and perhaps even gone crusading. At first the candidates for admission to one of the orders simply had to be freeborn and of legitimate birth. As with secular knights, however, the orders over time placed a greater emphasis on 'good' (i.e., noble) birth, by the thirteenth century requiring that new members be descendants of knights on their fathers' side. Nor were they admitted immediately without question. A prospective member of the order had to serve a period of noviciate, during which he learned the rules of the order and the officials in charge of his tutelage had ample opportunity to form an opinion about his character and worth. Only after he had proved himself as a novice, usually for a year, was a knight allowed to take the vows that bound him to the community for life.

Below: The military orders in the east made some adaptions to the climate, including dressing in Arab-style flowing robes and sometimes wearing turbans, like this Templar.

DECLINE AND TRANSFORMATION

The military religious orders were very much products of the crusades. The Crusader States fought a long rearguard action against resurgent Islam in the thirteenth century, the Mamluk rulers of Egypt finally taking the last outpost of the Kingdom of Jerusalem – Acre – in 1291.

Although the military orders committed themselves to a valiant defence of the city and few survived to tell the tale, after 1291 there was no longer a place for the monk-knights on the eastern shores of the Mediterranean, stripping them of their original purpose. By contrast, on the Iberian Peninsula and in the Baltic, the Knights in time suffered the consequences of their own success, once there were no more Muslim rulers or pagan Lithuanians to combat in the name of God.

The Latin Kingdom of Jerusalem only survived as long as it did because of the resources of the military orders. As in the twelfth century, in the thirteenth they invested enormously in defence of the frontier, and also continued to provide about half of the knights who fought under the royal banner in major battles, as well as employing many of the infantry. Their commitment could be costly. They – and the Kingdom of Jerusalem as a whole – suffered a catastrophic defeat in October 1244, when an invading force of Egyptians and Syrians, reinforced by Khwarezmian mercenaries, crushed the Christian army.

The knights of the orders fought doggedly, and only 33 Templars, 26 Hospitallers and 3 Teutonic Knights survived the engagement. Only a few years later, in 1250, the orders joined in full force

to support Louis IX of France's crusade against Egypt, only to be annihilated in the Battle of al-Mansurah; only three Templars and five Hospitallers with the army survived that engagement. By the second half of the thirteenth century, both Templar and Hospitaller finances were in a state of permanent crisis, as the cost of Holy Land defence continued to rise in face of the growing Mamluk menace to the south, while their revenues declined. Still they fought desperately to maintain at least a bridgehead for future crusades. In the doomed defence of Acre

in 1291, the marshals of both the Temple and the Hospital were killed, and both grand masters were mortally wounded.

THE FATE OF THE TEMPLARS

What next? The Teutonic Knights were in the most fortunate position after the fall of Acre, as they already had a new mission in the Baltic, which by then had already become their primary sphere of activity. For the next century, they continued to attract both recruits and crusaders, drawn by the chance to fight

Right: The charges brought against the Templars in 1307 included the bizarre claim that during their initiation new members were forced to trample and spit on the crucifix.

Left: King Louis IX on board a ship with his army during the Seventh Crusade (from an illuminated manuscript, 1450).

enemies of the faith. Their reason for existence was shattered in 1385, however, when Grand Duke Jogaila of Lithuania married the heiress of Poland, uniting the two lands in a personal union – and agreeing to accept baptism.

The conversion of the Lithuanians to Christianity proceeded rapidly, although the knights appear to have done their best to keep this news from spreading to the west. Nonetheless, crusaders gradually stopped appearing in Prussia, and in 1410 the order was defeated in a major battle by the Lithuanian-Polish confederation, the Battle of Tannenberg (or Grunwald). Most of the Teutonic Order's leaders were either killed or captured, although the survivors managed to withstand a siege of their great headquarters castle, Marienburg.

Right: The marriage of Jogaila of Lithuania and Jadwiga of Poland, shown here in a statue by Tomasz Sosnowski, united the Teutonic Knights' enemies against them.

Still, the order suffered some territorial loss, was forced to pay reparations, and never recovered the prestige it had lost. The end of the order in Prussia came in 1525, when Grand Master Albrecht von Hohenzollern converted to Protestantism and secularized the order's holdings, making himself the first duke of the new state of Prussia.

The fate of the Templars was not so benign. The period after the fall of Acre gave voice to increasingly strident calls for the reform of the military orders. Why did they not defend the Holy Land better, considering all the resources at their disposal? Commentators blamed the rivalry between the Templars and Hospitallers in particular for using up the orders'

energies when they should have been defending the last crusader outposts. Increasingly, members of the orders were also blamed for moral failings, not just the accusations of pride that had been flung at them for centuries, but also lust, greed and even cowardice. Some of these accusations may even have been true, as the Hospitallers and Templars both floundered for a

"Commentators blamed the rivalry between the Templars and Hospitallers in particular for using up the orders' energies when they should have been defending the last crusader outposts."

Left: The Battle of Tannenberg (1410) was a large engagement in which the Teutonic Order's forces were eventually overcome by the number of their enemies; most leaders of the Order were either killed or captured.

had not been an overwhelmingly formidable foe. For a few years, the Templars managed to maintain a force on the island of Arwad, just off the eastern Mediterranean coast, but a Mamluk army took this base after a short siege in 1302 or 1303. After that, the Templars appear to have cast around for a territory where they could form an independent state like that of the Teutonic Knights, but to no avail.

KING PHILIP IV
The Templars had always been a predominantly French order, with many of their commanderies in French territory and their new headquarters in Paris. Did King Philip IV of France fear the power of this well-armed and organized army within his territory, yet not subject to his rule? Did he covet the wealth and lands of the Templars? Or perhaps he really believed the stories that circulated of Templar misdeeds, not just personal lapses in morality but an order-wide

contempt of Christ, heresy and dabbling in witchcraft. Whatever his motivation, we know King Philip's action: on Friday 13 October 1307, he had all professed Knights Templars throughout his realm arrested, including their master, Jacques de Molay. The prisoners were tortured, and soon confessions emerged of how they spit on the cross during their profession, idolatry and other offences.

The king of France used the evidence received in this way to demand that the pope disband the order. Pope Clement V resisted royal pressure, demanding to hear from the arrested Templars themselves – many of whom then recanted their forced confessions. Still, the pope in Avignon was in a weak position, and dissolved the order in 1312. Many of the order's assets passed to the other military orders (although the king of France certainly profited), and many of the Templars transferred to other orders. Not Jacques de Molay, though. He retracted the confession he had made under torture and was burned in Paris as a relapsed heretic on 18 March 1314, on the pyre summoning both the king and the pope to meet him before God's judgment throne within the year.

number of years, seeking a mission that would give meaning to their lives when war against the Muslims in the Holy Land was simply no longer possible.

Jacques de Molay became grand master of the Temple in 1292. He worked tirelessly to encourage a new crusade, but the political and religious climate of Europe had changed, even if the Mamluks

"Pope Clement V resisted royal pressure, demanding to hear from the arrested Templars themselves – many of whom then recanted their forced confessions."

Facing page: Jacques de Molay and Geoffroi de Charnay (master of Normandy) were burned to death as heretics on March 18, 1314 in Paris after retracting the confessions they had made under torture.

Perhaps the happiest fate of the great military orders was that of the Knights of St John of the Hospital. They found a new purpose as a naval power patrolling the eastern Mediterranean and protecting pilgrims and merchants from Muslim corsairs, besides greatly hindering the advance of the Ottoman Turks into the Mediterranean. The Hospitallers took the island of Rhodes in a series of hard-fought campaigns between 1306 and 1310, developing it as a sovereign state. They proved to be a highly effective thorn in the side of the Ottoman sultan, who sent massive forces to besiege Rhodes in 1444–6 and again in 1480. They were forced out of Rhodes only in 1522, when the Ottoman Empire was at its height under Suleiman the Magnificent. Even then, they only moved as far as Malta, where they continued to wage stubborn war against both Turks and Muslim raiders from North Africa. They held Malta until 1798. Once again a purely hospitaller order, the headquarters of the Knights of Malta is now in Rome. Their few professed knights today still bear witness to the long history of the Hospitallers.

Left: Jacques de Molay, last grand master of the Temple. Historians still argue how much blame he should bear for his order's demise. Portrait by Amaury Duval Eugene.

ble maistre des templiers. Et com
mence ou latin. Actourtius · z̃·

Et viel; historiens dict
que aucuns religieu no
bles hommes sages et

Epilogue: The End of the Knight

The rulers of a number of countries still create knights. But in the modern world, the honour of knighthood has for the most part been detached from military prowess, which in the Middle Ages formed the core of the definition of knights. The transformation of the knight from heavy cavalryman to any individual, male or female, who renders special service to society was a gradual one, and the final stages in the process are not the concern of this book. The gradual erosion of a heavy cavalry united by a common code of behaviour and 'created' by a special act is, however, something that took place in the later Middle Ages and helps to mark the end of the era.

FROM KNIGHTS TO MEN-AT-ARMS

One of the first stages in the medieval decline of knighthood is that the number of knights began to decrease even while the vital function of heavy cavalry was still recognized on the battlefields of Europe. In part, this decline in numbers can be attributed to strong resistance to letting commoners break into the charmed circle of knighthood. We can see evidence of this caste mentality, for example, in the refusal of tournament organizers

Facing page: The creation of 59 new Knights of the Holy Sepulchre of Jerusalem in Paris, 2008. The order is devoted to religious and charitable work.

in the later Middle Ages to admit any competitor who could not certify his knightly bloodlines. But members of the knightly class themselves increasingly evaded the honour of knighthood as time went by, and it became more important to have the bloodlines to be *eligible* for knighthood than actually to receive the accolade.

Beginning in 1180, English kings tried to force qualified landowners to be knighted. For Henry II, the first king who attempted to enforce such a 'distraint of knighthood', the issue was that he needed more heavy cavalrymen and believed that men who held fiefs should remember that there was a military obligation attached to the estates they enjoyed. Henry's effort was limited to those who held fiefs in his French lands, where his warfare was incessant. In 1224, however,

his grandson Henry III ordered that all men among his subjects had to equip themselves as knights and receive the accolade if they held one or more knight's fees. By the end of the thirteenth century, King Edward I even provided eligible landowners with arms, apparently tired of excuses that they could not afford the cost of knighthood. England had only about 1500 knights at the time; of those, only about 500 were fit and of an age to take part in campaigns.

Some men eligible to become knights would have avoided the rank because they did not wish the expense of military service. Others simply preferred not to fight, instead paying a fee (*scutage*) to lawfully avoid military service. Some would have seen knighthood as a burden because of the non-military demands placed upon people of knightly

rank. In England, and to some extent in Germany and France, knights were heavily pressured to serve in local administration. By the mid-thirteenth century they were justices and served on juries. The feudal class – those knights who held estates conditionally in return for military service – was settling down rapidly to become country squires. They were less and less effective as a fighting force, especially as rulers so frequently preferred to take *scutage* instead of forcing their reluctant vassals on campaign. When a feudal summons was issued, it produced ever less result. England's last feudal summonses were in 1327 and 1385; in both cases, the returns were so meagre that the attempt was abandoned.

The men who filled the ranks of the heavy cavalry in the fourteenth and fifteenth centuries were still members of the social elite, since the equipment necessary to fight was prohibitively expensive. Some were still land-holding eldest sons, who for honour or loyalty chose to spend at least part of their adulthood in military

> *"...the accolade came to be granted more frequently as a reward for outstanding military service rather than at the outset of a military career."*

endeavours. Many more, however, were not fief-holders but younger sons who chose a military career to try to get ahead. Indeed, the always incomplete 'feudal system' hardly functioned at all by the fourteenth century, as the system of granting fiefs had given way to land purchases and unconditional ownership. Some would have sought the honour of knighthood, but the accolade came to be granted more frequently as a reward for outstanding military service rather than at the outset of a military career. For example, the French hero Bertrand du Guesclin (1320–80) was not knighted until he was thirty-four years old, after he had led troops (including knights) in battle for years.

Bertrand du Guesclin started his fighting career as a 'man-at-arms'. The term had emerged by the end of the thirteenth century to describe heavy cavalry, whether knights or not. Most of these men-at-arms were from

Above: A fifteenth-century French knight and his squire. The knight is equipped for jousting rather than war.

Right: Fifteenth-century men-at-arms and pikemen marching toward battle; both were necessary for military success.

reasonably good families, but anybody who could lay hands on the necessary armour and horses could serve as a man-at-arms. By the mid-fourteenth century, most men-at-arms were not knights. For example, in September 1340, Philip VI of France had around 28,000 men-at-arms serving in various theatres of war, but fewer than 3700 of them were knights – perhaps 12 per cent of his total heavy cavalry force. In the English army that opposed him, about a quarter of the heavy cavalry were knights. But by the time of Henry V's Agincourt campaign of 1415, knights comprised a mere 8% of the English cavalry force.

THE NEW AGE OF INFANTRY

As seen in Chapter 5, the growing effectiveness of infantry forces – pikemen and archers – has often been seen as a marker that the age of the knight (and of heavy cavalry in general) was at an end. Although infantry were responsible for a number of striking victories from about 1300, there was no dramatic change in how battles were fought at the time. Instead, what we see is a step in a trend. To be sure, a densely arrayed force of pikemen could stop a cavalry charge, as could carefully positioned massed archers. But the Anglo-Scottish wars that began at the turn of the fourteenth century (also known as

Right: The Battle of Stirling Bridge (1297). The best chance for infantry to succeed against knights was if they controlled the charge; here William Wallace took advantage of a narrow bridge.

"Philip VI of France had around 28,000 men-at-arms serving in various theatres of war, but fewer than 3700 of them were knights..."

the Scottish Wars of Independence) illustrate how complex the use of such forces could be, and ultimately demonstrate the ongoing importance of knights on the battlefield.

The Battle of Stirling Bridge, the great victory of the Scots under William Wallace in 1297, must have been a great shock to the English. It is usually hailed as a victory due to innovative Scottish use of infantry, although the poor judgment of the English commander also played a role. John de Warenne, Earl of Surrey, had already won a traditional victory in the Battle of Dunbar (1296), an engagement in which two heavy cavalry forces fought and the English men-at-arms overcame the Scots. This easy win may have given Surrey a low opinion of the Scottish

"Stirling Bridge demonstrated that – when conditions were right – infantry could defeat cavalry."

Below: William Wallace, a Scot of knightly family, was King John Balliol's steward. When John was imprisoned in England and Edward I assumed direct control, Wallace became a resistance leader.

'rebels', making him display an overconfidence that the Scots exploited at Stirling.

The key to the engagement on 11 September 1297 was the bridge, a narrow span that only two men-at-arms abreast could cross at a time. Surrey recognized the difficulty and camped on the south side of the river for several days, attempting to negotiate. Finally, he forced the issue, sending his heavy cavalry across in a manoeuvre that took several hours. When about 2000 of his men-at-arms were on the north side, Scots spearmen attacked them, cutting off the bridge so no English reinforcements could reach the outnumbered men and then assaulting the stranded Englishmen from all directions. With no room to build up speed for a charge, the English lost the advantage of the impact that made a knightly charge so irresistible, and the tight clusters of Scots spearmen gradually brought down the enemy horses, rendering the men-at-arms they bore vulnerable. Most of the 2000 or so men-at-arms on the north side of the river were killed, either in direct enemy action or by drowning.

Stirling Bridge demonstrated that – when conditions were right – infantry could defeat cavalry. But an essential feature of the battle was that the English men-at-arms were largely stationary and under attack by the infantrymen, the tactics of the Scots general having neutralized the threat of the dreaded cavalry charge.

Facing page: Robert the Bruce (King of Scotland 1306–1329) was a brilliant strategist and tactician who effectively drove the English from Scotland.

William Wallace thought he had developed an effective way to ward off English cavalry, but was proven to be mistaken at the Battle of Falkirk in the following year. In this great battle, fought on 22 July 1298, Wallace commanded a predominantly infantry force, while King Edward I led about 2500 men-at-arms in addition to a large contingent of infantry. Wallace did not evade the battle, but took position with a wood to his rear, arraying his pikemen in four dense circular formations (*schiltrons*), with archers placed between the schiltrons and his thousand men-at-arms to the rear, where they could be sent to where they were needed in the heat of battle.

The Scots archers appear to have been unprotected by stakes or ditches to impede a cavalry charge, and indeed they were soon overrun and destroyed when Edward sent his cavalry against them. The Scots cavalry did charge their English counterparts, but soon realized they were badly outnumbered and abandoned the field. The schiltrons by contrast held firm, presenting an impenetrable shield wall. Most Scots infantrymen were not armed as well as the Anglo-Saxon warriors who had formed the shield wall at Hastings in 1066, but the long pikes they carried – so the whole formation bristled like a porcupine – provided a new advantage, since the men-at-arms could not get close enough

> ## "…the death of Edward I of England replaced one of the great commanders of the Middle Ages with his weak and ineffectual son."

Above: At a key point of the Battle of Bannockburn (1314) the Scottish *schiltrons* advanced in tight formation against the English, killing many and driving many more into the stream at their back.

to strike at their enemies. King Edward had too much sense to launch his heavy cavalry against such an unpromising target, so he borrowed a tactic from William the Conqueror and instead sent in archers. As at Hastings, the archers wreaked havoc among their opponents, although at Falkirk the damage they inflicted would have been much quicker and more devastating: Edward had more archers than William had commanded at Hastings, they were armed with the more powerful longbow, and the Scots had less protective armour. When enough men in each schiltron were wounded or dead, the English king sent his cavalry in a charge to break up the formation completely. William Wallace escaped the carnage and attempted a guerrilla campaign against the English, but was captured and executed.

THE CHARGE AS INEFFECTIVE TACTIC

The Scots soon rallied under Robert the Bruce, and the death of Edward I of England replaced one of the great commanders of the Middle Ages with his weak and ineffectual son. Robert (who was crowned as king of the Scots in 1306) began the long process of driving the occupying English from Scotland, taking fortresses with a series of ruses and sudden attacks. Stirling Castle, however, proved to be a much harder target. King Robert settled down to a siege while the garrison urgently appealed to King Edward II for military assistance.

The English king brought a large army to the relief of Stirling Castle, which met and was defeated by a smaller, infantry-dominated Scottish force at the Battle of Bannockburn south of Stirling, fought on 23–24 June 1314. The Scots adopted a strong defensive position similar to that of the Flemings at Courtrai, with densely arrayed schiltrons of pikemen placed behind the stream that gave the battle its name and with pits dug in front of them to impede a cavalry charge still further. After minor cavalry engagements on the first day of the battle, the English succeeded in crossing the stream during the night, but the ground before them was still unsuitable for a cavalry charge. Yet charge they did, nonetheless. The story behind this disastrous move was that two earls with the English army, the earls of Gloucester and Hereford, had a quarrel over which of them had the right to lead the vanguard. Hereford accused Gloucester of cowardice, which led Gloucester to prove his courage by launching a full frontal charge against the Scottish pikemen. Unsurprisingly, his charge failed, and Gloucester died along with many of his men. The English longbowmen, who should have opened the engagement, then began shooting to try to support their men-at-arms, but were ordered to stop because some of their arrows were inflicting casualties among the men-at-arms who were still engaged. Some longbowmen then attempted to break up the *schiltron* from a flank position, but they were scattered by a Scottish cavalry charge. The English cavalry, too tightly packed together in a constrained space, was not able

Below: Morale is fundamental resisting a heavy cavalry charge. The Scots at Bannockburn had an inspiring and charismatic leader in King Robert.

to manoeuvre; when the Scots pikemen advanced, they were unable to hold their position. The result was a catastrophic defeat for the English under their hapless king, who was dragged away to safety by his bodyguard.

INFANTRY RIVALLING CAVALRY

What did Bannockburn teach, besides the fact that Edward II was a poor general? It displayed yet

Below: The English garrison in Stirling Castle had vowed to surrender to the Scots unless they were relieved by mid-summer. True to his word, the commander refused to admit the defeated Edward II to the castle and turned it over to Robert the Bruce.

again that infantry *could* triumph over traditional heavy cavalry – if the conditions were right. One should note, however, that the Scots cavalry played a significant role in the engagement. So perhaps this famous battle should be taken rather as evidence of a new age of integrated infantry-cavalry forces, which failed because of poor tactics in the case of the English and succeeded brilliantly for the Scots.

The Battle of Bannockburn showed the new risks of cavalry charges against well-placed, densely formed infantry, but it by no means signalled an end to the usefulness of knights and their lesser-ranked men-at-arms in battle. It took until the reign of Edward II had ended – in

deposition and probable murder – for the English to avenge their defeat at Bannockburn, but the revenge when it came must have been sweet. In two major battles – Dupplin Moor (1332) and Halidon Hill (1333) – English forces destroyed two Scots armies. In these battles we see the English employing new tactics that soon proved to be so effective in the Hundred Years' War, assuming a defensive position with dismounted men-at-arms stiffening the resistance of longbowmen who were stationed on the flanks. In the

Facing page: The Battle of Halidon Hill (1333). The Scots, more lightly armed, stood little chance against the dismounted English men-at-arms.

first battle, a mixed Anglo-Scottish force led by Edward Balliol tried to claim the throne of Scotland from its child-king David. The badly led national Scottish force attempted to charge Balliol's position, only to be thrown into disorder by the English archery. At Halidon Hill

Below: In the Battle of Homildon Hill (1402), the Scots army was largely destroyed with archery fire; when a small number attempted still to charge the English position, the longbowmen dropped their bows and engaged with swords and daggers.

in the following year, Edward III of England again dismounted his men-at-arms and positioned archers on the flanks. When the Scots attacked over marshy ground, they were annihilated.

The battles of the Scottish War for Independence display a number of tactics, with first one side and then the other relying more on cavalry, as well as one or both sides making greater and sometimes devastatingly effective use of infantry formations. One looks in vain for a 'secret weapon' that could assure victory; rather

the pikemen and archers deployed in these battles were only two of the options in the full toolbox of tactical options available to the commanders. These battles perhaps best display the growing complexity of generalship in the later Middle Ages, as commanders strove to use an array of forces as effectively as possible against their enemies.

Nonetheless, the Anglo-Scots battles were revolutionary in one regard: like other battles of the fourteenth century, they were astonishingly bloody when compared to their counterparts in the thirteenth century. Shockingly, many more men-at-arms were dying in battle. The reasons for this transformation are not hard to find: arrows have no respect for rank, and many commoners, with their inferior armour, fell prey to them. Among the knightly class, arrows must have caused many a fall from a wounded, pain-crazed horse, and in the engagements of the fourteenth century many men-at-arms must have been ridden over by their own comrades in the heat of battle. If they tumbled close to the enemy line, the men they faced could not afford to show mercy, because once on his feet again a man-at-arms could do significant damage even if dismounted. The same was true of pikemen: in order to survive themselves, they had to completely incapacitate their dismounted foes.

As it became increasingly frequent for fighters of the knightly class to engage seriously with commoners – not just brushing them aside in panicked flight but assaulting them repeatedly

against tough resistance, as was the case at Crécy or Agincourt – the long-established tradition of taking captives for ransom also largely broke down. Common foot soldiers could not pay ransoms, so men-at-arms showed little compunction about killing them. Even if men-at-arms attacked well-armed members of their own social class, as when the French knights at Poitiers confronted dismounted English men-at-arms, the close-order fighting made it harder to take captives.

CLASS WARFARE

When they came against commoners, the infantry sometimes appear to have

Above: The Battle of Poitiers, as depicted in the *Grandes Chroniques de France* (c. 1415). The knights are wearing pig-snout bascinets.

delighted in slaughtering their 'betters'. For example, at the Battle of Courtrai in 1302, the Flemish pikemen against whom the French charged had every reason

"They ambushed the Austrian force, throwing rocks onto Leopold's men-at-arms in the narrow defile below them..."

to be sure that their foes were neutralized, but at breaks in the action they went to fallen knights and administered the *coup de grâce* rather than taking prisoners, until

by the end of the day between 40 and 50% of the French cavalry lay dead. Such actions suggest a strong element of class antipathy.

The Swiss who defeated Duke Leopold of Austria at Morgarten in 1315 appear to have felt a similar combination of fear and animosity. They ambushed the Austrian force, throwing rocks onto Leopold's men-at-arms in the narrow defile below them, then slaughtered the Hapsburgers with their halberds. By contrast, at the Battle of Bouvines in 1214, fewer than 200 of the allied knights died in battle, and only two heavy cavalrymen on the French side fell that day.

Even when taken prisoner, the old rules of courteous treatment increasingly broke down in the

face of a new military pragmatism. The Swiss and Flemings both killed knightly prisoners, as did Sultan Bayezid after the Battle of Nicopolis in 1396. Perhaps these cases are not surprising, since in the first two instances commoners were dealing with hated and feared members of the supposedly superior military caste and in the third the Ottoman Turks were victorious over enemies of their faith. But what are we to make of Henry V's order to kill prisoners at the Battle of Agincourt in 1415? In this instance, the king feared the approach of a new French force, and did not trust his large number of noble prisoners not to turn on him when they saw a chance of victory. That lack of trust was in

Left: The Battle of Morgarten (1315) was part of a war of Swiss independence from Hapsburg rule, in which Swiss infantrymen won a reputation for slaughtering knights.

Below: In the Battle of La Roche-Derrien (1347) Duke Charles of Brittany suffered an embarrassing defeat at the hands of an English force of longbowmen and was captured.

"...the most famous case of such a landless knight making good is William Marshal, who ended his life as Earl of Pembroke."

itself a sign of changing times, since it was probably with good reason that he did not expect his captives to do the honourable thing if opportunity presented itself. Interestingly, though, Henry's own men-at-arms refused to carry out his orders. They knew that it was dishonourable to kill prisoners, at least those of comparable rank. So Henry had his archers dispatch the French captives, which they did by clubbing them over the head (apparently they had been

unhelmed, but still wore their heavy armour).

Battles also became more frequent as fourteenth-century leaders engaged larger infantry forces. Infantrymen were cheaper and quicker to train than men-at-arms, as well as being available in larger numbers. They also seem to have created a new confidence that made their commanders willing to engage in battle, while also inspiring the enemy commander with the belief that his knightly force could

take on a rabble of commoners. It is startling to note that there were nineteen major battles in western Europe in the period 1302–1347 – more than had taken place in the preceding 200 years.

THE AGE OF MERCENARIES

Some heavy cavalrymen had always fought for pay, but in the first centuries of knighthood the ideal remained the landed knight who gave loyal military service to his lord in return for the fief he was granted. Even when the majority of knights were younger sons serving in the households of lords, they still dreamed of the day they would be given the estate that would make it possible to settle and raise a family; the most famous case of such a landless knight making good is William Marshal, who ended his life as Earl of Pembroke.

Facing page: William Marshal led the barons of England in revolt against King John, but when John died became regent for his young son, Henry III and pacified the kingdom.

Right: A *condottiere*, by the painter and sculptor Frederic Leighton.

By around 1300, the way heavy cavalrymen were recruited for campaigns was beginning to change, a process speeded by the frequent conflicts of the Hundred Years' War, as well as perennial warfare in Spain, Italy and Germany. Some men continued to fight because they held fiefs and felt a sense of obligation to their lord, although the legal requirement to answer a feudal summons was abandoned in the early fourteenth century and they received pay for their service. Others continued to find a place in a military household, serving a single lord for years or even decades, a lord who still felt honour-bound to fight (either to serve his king or in private wars with the neighbours). Many others were contract workers, hired for a year or the duration of a particular campaign, recruited by military leaders who in turn had made agreements to provide a fixed number of men with particular stipulations about equipment.

Men-at-arms who served by contractual agreement are often known as *condottieri* after the *condotta* or contract that they signed, the Italian term gaining general currency because they were so prevalent in Italy. These mercenary fighters could be found in most areas of Europe, and their excesses tarnished the image of how a well-bred heavy cavalryman ought to behave. But then some of them were anything but well bred. The requirement to be taken on in a *condotta* was not noble blood, but the proper equipment and an ability to fight. Some of the greatest *condottieri* were of surprisingly common birth; for example, the father of Sir John Hawkwood seems to have been a tanner by trade, although he owned enough land to equip his son.

Mercenary companies already inspired fear in the late twelfth century, when the French *routiers* were noted for their brutality. These bands, mostly infantry but led by knights, were so hated for their tendency to pillage and rape at will that they were condemned by the Third Lateran Council; King John of England's use of mercenaries contributed so strongly to his unpopularity that they were specifically banned by Magna Carta in 1215.

THE FIRST COMPANY OF MERCENARIES

The wars of the thirteenth century did not encourage the formation of mercenary bands, but they returned with a vengeance in the wars between Aragon and Sicily at the end of the century. When the decades of fighting between these two lands finally ended, many fighting men were left unemployed. This led to the formation of the first major mercenary company of the late Middle Ages, the Catalan

Grand Company. It became the model, both in organization and in aspiration, for later mercenary bands. The Catalan Grand Company's founder was a military adventurer named Roger de Flor (1267–1305), who started life with the impediment of illegitimacy (he was the son of an Italian noblewoman and a German falconer) but won success as a pirate. His naval abilities led to an invitation to enter the service of the king of Sicily. When peace came in

Below: The entry of Roger de Flor into Constantinople. A mural in the Palacio del Senado de España, Madrid.

Left: Federico da Montefeltro (1422–1482) was one of the most successful *condottieri* of all time, who seized the duchy of Urbino and ruled it until his death. He always had himself shown in profile in art, to disguise the loss of an eye in battle.

1302, Roger was in a predicament, not willing to give up his position or the men he commanded. So the Grand Company – a mixed force of about 1500 men-at-arms and 4000 foot soldiers – set out for the east. They took service with the Byzantine emperor, who showed how badly he needed the support of this fresh blood by permitting Roger de Flor to marry his niece.

The Catalan Grand Company soon came into conflict with the Genoese, who dominated the Byzantine state at the time. Roger and his men continued to fight for the emperor in Turkey for a while, but soon the emperor learned to fear this powerful and uncontrollable force. The emperor's son ordered another mercenary group to murder Roger de Flor and his men, arranging a great banquet

as cover for the deed in 1305. Roger did fall in the attack, as did at least 1100 men of the Grand Company. The rest exacted a brutal revenge on the populace of Gallipoli, and then went freelance. They decided to carve out a state for themselves in Greece, taking Athens in 1311. The Catalan Grand Company continued to rule the duchies of Athens and Neopatras in Greece until the end of the century.

Other *condottieri* moved freely between the campaigns of the Hundred Years' War and the constant fighting between the small states of northern Italy. The Italians, with their wealth and grievous quarrels (Bologna and Modena fought a war in 1325 over a bucket that Modenese soldiers stole from a town well), were ideal employers. As a result, at the same time that heavy cavalry was being battered in the set-piece battles of the Hundred Years' War in France, they were receiving a new lease on life in Italy. Most of the men-at-arms who fought in this way are nameless. Many were German; more than 700 German cavalry leaders have been identified as active in Italy in the period 1320–60, with as many as 10,000 men-at-arms at their command. An interesting example of the breed is the mercenary captain Werner von Urslingen (1308–54). Werner was the younger son of a duke. With few prospects at home, he went to make a name for himself,

"Other condottieri *moved freely between the campaigns of the Hundred Years' War and the constant fighting between the small states of northern Italy."*

The Mercenary John Hawkwood

One of the most interesting of these knightly mercenaries was John Hawkwood (1320–94). A younger son who appears to have fought at first as a longbowman, Hawkwood was probably with the English force at both Crécy and Poitiers. When peace broke out with the signing of the Treaty of Brétigny in 1360, he became a mercenary, having no other means of support. He joined the White Company, founded by a German captain in 1361 to fight in Italy. Hawkwood was elected its leader in 1363. By that time he appears to have fought as a heavy cavalryman, and in later life was designated as a knight, although it is unknown when or where he received the honour, if indeed he did; many *condottiere* men-at-arms were called 'knight' with a fine lack of social distinction. Hawkwood led his men to a series of victories when in the service of Florence, often employing English tactics with careful placement of archers and dismounted men-at-arms. When he died in 1394, Florence gave their loyal mercenary captain a fine marble tomb in the Duomo. A century later, the English writer William Caxton held up the great *condottiere* as a model of chivalry.

Right: This fresco of the *condottiere* John Hawkwood was painted above his tomb in the Duomo of Florence by Paolo Uccello.

"Werner used his status and fighting reputation to attract men to his own Great Company..."

joining the Company of St George, which, when it was founded in 1339, was the first large mercenary company in Italy. Within three years, Werner used his status and fighting reputation to attract men to his own Great Company, which entered the service of a number of cities and princes, often accepting bribes to change sides, ravaging the countryside, and winning a reputation for rapacity and anarchy. Werner appears to have delighted in this dark side of knighthood, wearing black armour that had his motto inscribed on the breastplate: 'Enemy of God, Pity, and Mercy'.

Men like Werner von Urslingen largely abandoned the code of chivalry, leading their lives in camps, not only mauling peasants but those of a high enough rank that they expected to be safe from honourable knights, even attacking priests and churches. Other *condottieri*, however, did aspire to live in accordance with contemporary notions of chivalry, and used their military contracts as stepping stones to knighthood, public honours, and even rule of one of the Italian principalities. Such men fulfilled their contracts as promised, and by means of courtesy and generosity even won the affection of the citizens they were hired to protect.

THE END OF CHIVALRY?

By the fifteenth century, it is easy to find examples of 'unknightly' knights, rough or pragmatic soldiers in heavy armour who were clearly out for profit and didn't mind letting the world see it. Men like Sir John Fastolf (1380–1459) had no romantic appeal; they were not of noble blood and did not compensate by adopting the chivalric code of behaviour. People like Fastolf, who invested the profits of war wisely instead of behaving with courteous generosity, were common enough; so were the battlefield executions of noble enemies that so marred the English Wars of the Roses in the second half of the fifteenth century. Yet, as the case of John Hawkwood demonstrates, the code of chivalry was far from dead, and there were probably many more Hawkwoods even among the *condottieri* than there were men like Werner von Urslingen. After all, there were few mercenary captains so hard-bitten that they did not want esteem and admiration, and to gain that they had to act in accordance with the chivalric code.

The fifteenth century and well into the sixteenth was still permeated with chivalry. Books, both fiction and non-fiction, on chivalric topics continued to reach broad audiences; works like Christine de Pizan's *The Book of Deeds of Arms and of Chivalry* (1410) and a continuing flow of vernacular romances. Such works complained that contemporary knights had lost vigour and become effete, but that charge had already

Right: Sir John Fastolf (1380–1459) was not particularly chivalrous, which may have inspired Shakespeare's parody in the character Sir John Falstaff.

Facing page: A tournament, fought in a Flemish town square in the early sixteenth century. Special stands were constructed for spectators.

been levied against knights by authors in the twelfth century. Authors were more likely to celebrate the nobility of chivalric ideals, in works ranging from Thomas Malory's *Morte d'Arthur* (first printed in 1485) to Ariosto's *Orlando Furioso* (1532), to Spencer's *Faerie Queene* of 1590. The work of the early printing presses shows how eager audiences were to devour such work; for instance, the first book printed in England was the romance *History of Troy* (1474). Tournaments also continued through the sixteenth

century, elaborate and fantastical celebrations of chivalry that were increasingly divorced from actual battlefield fighting; Henry II of France was killed in a joust in 1559. And one should not forget that rulers continued to knight men for outstanding service. In 1581, Elizabeth I knighted Francis Drake on the deck of his *Golden Hind* when he returned to England from circumnavigating the globe.

The notion of the perfect knight had great staying power. The Burgundian Jacques de Lalaing, who died in 1453, was

Above: Sir John Chandos was mortally wounded in a minor skirmish at Lussac in 1369 after he tripped on his long surcoat.

regarded as an ideal knight; his professed goal was to fight thirty men in jousts by the time he reached the age of thirty. He was not just a tournament knight, though; de Lalaing also had a distinguished military career.

One of the most highly regarded knights of all time was Pierre de Terrail, the Chevalier de Bayard (1473–1524), praised as

The Tenth Worthy

The French general Bertrand du Guesclin (1323–80) shows how even a mercenary career of the later Middle Ages could be shaped by chivalry. Du Guesclin, the younger son of a minor knightly family, began his military adventures as a *routier* captain in the early stages of the Hundred Years' War. He soon proved his worth as a commander and was knighted for his loyal service to the French crown in 1354, going on to become constable of France. He profited greatly from his legendary military skill, but his contemporary biography does not emphasize that point. Instead, the anonymous author lauds his hero's consideration for ladies, his courtesy towards his peers, and his outstanding generosity. Bertrand du Guesclin lived up to chivalry as his contemporaries imagined it, even when it was not in his best military interest. For example, when he was captured in an engagement, the Black Prince said that du Guesclin could set the amount of his own ransom; to satisfy his honour, the captive knight named an exorbitant amount – which his king paid for him. When du Guesclin died of illness while on campaign in Languedoc, foes as well as friends mourned his demise, and King Charles V ordered his burial among the kings of France in the monastery church of St-Denis.

Bertrand du Guesclin was hailed as the 'Tenth Worthy', a knight so great that he should be set alongside the nine legendary heroes of the ancient and medieval worlds. Other knights of the late Middle Ages also continued to be honoured

Above: The death of Bertrand du Guesclin while besieging Chateauneuf-de-Randon in 1380. As Constable of France, he had defeated the English many times.

as paragons of chivalry in terms that made it clear that such a man could bask in the adulation of his contemporaries. The historian Jean Froissart reports, for instance, that du Guesclin's contemporary, the English commander and diplomat Sir John Chandos (c. 1320–69),

was the most courteous knight alive. Like his French counterpart, Chandos was of modest birth and rose to prominence thanks to his military skill. Also like du Guesclin, Chandos' death in a minor engagement was mourned by both sides.

H.Ford. 1917.

a peerless, blameless knight and honoured as a hero of the Franco–Italian wars of the early sixteenth century. Both his courtesy and his fighting skill were legendary; he once held a bridge against a force of two hundred Spanish knights. Perhaps the pinnacle of the Chevalier de Bayard's career came in 1515 when he was asked to knight his young king, Francis I.

THE END OF THE MEDIEVAL KNIGHT

The creation of new, national armies in the later fifteenth century struck a blow against the special prestige of knighthood, since they ended the contract system of recruitment and paid the same wages to knights as to other men-at-arms. But heavy cavalrymen still played an important role, even though

the size of cavalry contingents declined in relation to other forces arrayed on Europe's battlefields. For example, Duke Charles the Bold of Burgundy's armies in the 1470s were organized by 'lances'. Each lance consisted of a man-at-arms (the only one of the team who actually carried a lance into battle), a page, an armed servant, three mounted archers, a crossbowman and a handgunner. All had a role to play.

Duke Charles lost a series of battles in 1476 and 1477 in which victory is usually ascribed to Swiss pikemen, trained to a lethal degree and wielding pikes up to 5.5m (18ft) long. The reality, though, was that both sides deployed mixed forces, except at the Battle of Granson (1476), where the Swiss did not have cavalry and so were unable to follow up their victory by pursuing the fleeing Burgundians. The Battles of Morat and Nancy were more decisive because of the role of Swiss cavalry, Charles of Burgundy suffering a decisive defeat and losing his life in the latter.

What really marked the end of the distinctive knightly style of fighting – as heavy cavalry – was the gradual improvement over two centuries of gunpowder technology. No single invention or innovation was decisive, but their cumulative effect by the late sixteenth century had eroded the battlefield effectiveness of heavy cavalry to the point where generals and fighting men alike gave up the practice. Up until the 1570s, however, heavy cavalry continued to play an important role in battle.

King Edward III brought several small cannons to the battlefield of Crécy in 1346, but they played no useful role unless they succeeded in startling some enemy horses. Their failure was hardly surprising; early cannon could not be aimed, were very slow to load and fire, and until the method of corning gunpowder was developed in the late fourteenth century did not hurl a projectile with great power. By the early fifteenth century, cannons were proving their usefulness against stationary targets, like town walls, but their slowness and heaviness made them more of a liability than a help on the battlefield. Even though a hand cannon soon developed, its slowness and cumbersomeness limited its use to sieges.

> *"King Edward III brought several small cannon to the battlefield of Crécy in 1346, but they played no useful role unless they succeeded in startling some enemy horses."*

The first half of the fifteenth century saw some developments that presaged the gunpowder superiority to come. The key to effective gun use in their early years was to provide enough protection for the guns and their gunners, rather like the protection given to English longbowmen in the battles of Crécy, Poitiers or Agincourt. The Hussite heretics of Bohemia came up with a highly effective tactic that allowed them to hold out against three knight-

dominated crusades in the 1420s and 30s. They deployed war wagons, loaded with crossbows, hand culverins and cannon, making temporary fortresses on the battlefield by chaining several of these wagons together, and unloading the cannons between

Below: Charles the Bold's flight after his army was routed at the Battle of Granson (1476). Charles' dream of uniting his territories led to his own eventual death in battle.

"The French army at Castillon had... an intelligent ordinance officer who constructed an artillery park, protecting his guns behind a deep trench and an earthwork."

them so they could be fired at the enemy. This practice created consternation among their enemies but was not widely imitated.

Another sign of changing times was the last great engagement of the Hundred Years' War, the Battle of Castillon, on 17 July 1453. Charles VII of France ordered the invasion of English-held Guyenne, an invasion that had at its core the king's new standing army and state-of-the-art ordinance. The French army at Castillon had perhaps 300 cannon with it and an intelligent ordinance officer who constructed an artillery park, protecting his guns behind a deep trench and an earthwork. The English commander, Sir John Talbot, made a fatal miscalculation, thinking that the French were retreating and ordering an attack. Despite soon learning his mistake, he continued to commit his army piecemeal as they arrived on the field, sending them in hopeless charges against the well-protected French artillery. The battle has aptly been described as 'Crécy in reverse'. Talbot and as many as 4000 of his men were killed, and the French were able to take Guyenne.

It took another century before gunfire was effective enough to bring an end to the heavy cavalry charge. True, a cannon could rip a person apart even if he was wearing plate armour, and improved gun construction made it increasingly likely that a bullet from an arquebus would pierce plate. Several great late medieval knights were killed by gunfire, as we have already seen was the fate of Sir John Talbot at Castillon. Jacques de Lalaing was killed by a cannon ball at a siege in the same year, and in 1524 the Chevalier Bayard fell to an arquebus ball.

Above: A cannon of the type Edward III brought to the Battle of Crécy. These early gunpowder weapons were slow, weak, and often more deadly to their own side than the enemy.

Facing page: The death of John Talbot, earl of Shrewsbury, at the Battle of Castillon, painted by Charles-Philippe Larivière (1838).

Such injuries became more frequent as improvements in gunsmithing made it possible to fire gunpowder weapons more quickly and effectively.

Finally, by the end of the sixteenth century, cavalrymen abandoned the heavy armour that was the most distinctive feature of the medieval knight, although some units continued to wear just breastplates until well into the nineteenth century. But they were no longer knights and, once and for all, the honour of knighthood was detached from membership in a military elite whose members fought in a distinctive style as heavy cavalry.

Glossary

accolade: the ceremony of conferring knighthood, performed by striking a blow with a sword or the flat of a hand

Almohads: an Islamic caliphate founded in Morocco in the twelfth century, which expanded to rule all of Muslim Spain; their hold of Spain was lost soon after their defeat at the Battle of Las Navas de Tolosa in 1212

arming cap: a felted cloth cap worn under a coif and helmet to provide a better fit and help buffer blows to the head

arquebus: a long-barrelled hand gun developed in the fifteenth century; at first fired with a match, a matchlock mechanism and trigger were later added

arrêt de cuirasse: a bracket to hold the lance steady when in the horizontal position, riveted to the breastplate

banneret: a knight honoured with command over a unit of 12–20 men; he had the right to bear a square banner instead of the usual triangular pennon

barding: horse armour, usually stiffened leather or later metal plates covering at least the horse's hindquarters

bascinet: a helmet style popular in the fourteenth century, usually with a moveable visor

battle (also known as *échelle, constabularium, conrois,* or *bataille*): a large force of knights or men-at-arms; a typical battlefield tactic was to divide the cavalry into two or three 'battles' that could charge the enemy successively

cantle: the back part of a saddle; for knights the cantle was usually high to help hold them in the saddle during the impact of a charge

Carolingians: the royal dynasty that ruled the Kingdom of the Franks from 751; the dynasty ended in Germany in 911 and in France in 987

Cathars: dualist heretics, active in southern France and northern Italy in the twelfth and thirteenth centuries; the Albigensian Crusade was called to supress them

chanson de geste: a 'song of deeds,' these epic tales of the late eleventh and twelfth centuries told of deeds of great knights, especially figures associated with Charlemagne

chausses: leg armour, introduced for knights in the twelfth century; at first made of mail, they were later plate armour

chivalry: a band of knights, the method of fighting as knights, or above all the code of behaviour expected of knights, with emphasis on loyalty, generosity, and courage

Cistercians: an order of monks founded in 1098; although dedicated to a return to the original Benedictine Rule, the Cistercians also sponsored such innovations as the military religious orders

coif: a mail hood, which could be worn either on its own or under a helmet

condotta: a contract for mercenary service, above all in Italy

condottiere: a mercenary hired by means of a *condotta*

courtly love: an idealized and highly stylized set of rules for how knights ought to love ladies

courts of love: perhaps fictional, Andreas Capellanus popularized the idea that actual semi-legal process would rule on questions of proper behaviour in courtly love

crossbow: a heavy, short bow fixed on a stock; the cord was pulled by inserting one or both feet in a stirrup and then pulling back, later with a winch mechanism; the quarrel was then released with a trigger mechanism

crusades: a series of wars beginning in 1095, above all to win or protect Jerusalem for Christians, but also expanding to include wars against heretics, the pope's enemies, and the Ottoman Turks

culverin: either a small cannon or a hand culverin, in both cases a simple smoothbore tube, fired by inserting a match into the touchhole

destrier: the preferred war horse of the later Middle Ages, also known as the 'great horse'; destriers were large, stocky horses, with short backs

distraint of knighthood: a legal device forcing eligible landowners to receive the order of knighthood

dubbing: the act of making a knight by means of a blow with open hand or the flat of a sword

excommunication: a church sanction, imposed by the pope or a bishop, denying a person access to the sacraments

feudal summons: a call-up of all knights who owe military service in return for holding a fief; traditionally the knights were expected to serve for 40 days without pay

feudal system: the grant of estates to knights conditionally in return for military and other services; never consistent, but many twelfth- and thirteenth-century knights held such conditional grants

fief: also known as a fee, the grant of land made to a knight in return for military and other service

gorget: neck armour

Grail: a holy cup or chalice beloved in medieval romances; it was believed to be the cup Jesus used at the Last

Supper, later brought to England by Joseph of Arimathea

great helm: a thirteenth-century helmet made in a single piece that covered the head completely

hauberk: also known as a haubergeon, a shirt of chain mail reaching to mid-thigh or knee

Hussites: followers of the preacher Jan Hus of Bohemia, who was condemned for heresy in 1415; the Hussites staged a nationalist, religious revolution in Bohemia and successfully fought off three anti-Hussite crusades in the early fifteenth century

jongleur: a wandering minstrel and story-teller

joust: a competition between two mounted knights, who would attempt to unhorse each other using blunted lances

laminated armour: strips of metal riveted together in an overlapping pattern to protect joints

lance: a heavy spear, braced underarm by a charging knight; in the late Middle Ages, the term could also refer to a fighting team consisting of a man-at-arms, a squire, and a number of bowmen, pikemen, or gunners

longbow: a simple bow, usually crafted of yew; English longbows were six feet or longer and could have a pull of over 100 pounds

loricati: literally 'armoured men', this term was used in Latin sources of the tenth and eleventh centuries to refer to proto-knights

Magyars: Hungarians; originally nomadic tribesmen from the steppe whose mounted raids devastated eastern and central Europe in the late ninth and tenth centuries

mail: flexible armour made of interlinked iron rings

man-at-arms: the term used from c. 1300 onwards to describe any heavy cavalryman, whether he had been knighted or not

melée: a fight between two groups of fighting men, whether in battle or at a tournament

miles: one of several medieval words for a fighting man, by the tenth century it had come to mean a mounted heavy cavalryman; by c. 1150 a *miles* was a knight

military religious order: a religious organisation whose members take permanent vows to lead a monastic life that includes a military mission, such as defense of the Kingdom of Jerusalem

ministeriales: serf-knights, common in Germanic lands until the mid-twelfth century; they had many of the privileges of knights in other regions, but were legally unfree and subject to their lord's pleasure

minnesinger: literally a 'love singer', minnesingers were the German equivalent of troubadours

order of chivalry: an exclusive 'club' of knights, usually formed by a prince or king to honour outstanding knights

Ottonians: the dynasty that ruled Germany and northern Italy from 918 to 1024

page: a boy being trained to be a knight, tasked with serving his lord's household

pattern-welding: an early medieval sword-making process that consisted of twisting and beating together a number of fine iron rods, creating a flexible yet strong blade

pavise: a large shield used by crossbowmen; they would normally fight in pairs, one sheltering them with the pavise while the other fired

pell: a sturdy post against which knights in training would practice their sword work

pike: a long, sturdy spear, by the late Middle Ages sometimes as long as eighteen feet; especially used as protection against cavalry charges

quintain: a vertical post with a swiveling horizontal beam on one side of which was a shield and on the other a weighted sack; in training, knights had to strike the shield with their lance while avoiding the sack

romance: a story told in the vernacular language about the deeds of knights and their ladies; the genre developed in the middle of the twelfth century

Round Table: in the Arthurian legend, the table around which King Arthur and his finest knights met; it was the prototype for orders of chivalry

routiers: mercenary soldiers, organised into bands or *routes*, which gave them their name; the term first appears in the twelfth century

sabaton: foot armour

sallet: a visored helmet with a tail to protect the neck, popular in the fifteenth century

schiltron: a tightly ordered infantry formation, used especially to describe Scottish pikemen of the late thirteenth and fourteenth centuries

scutage: a payment in place of military service owed to a lord

shaffron: horse head armour

shield wall: a densely-arrayed stationary infantry formation

spangenhelm: an early medieval helmet, covering the top of the head and often with a nasal guard

squire: an aspirant to knighthood, old enough to fight but not yet dubbed a knight

surcoat: a sleeveless garment worn over armour, typically decorated with the wearer's coat of arms

tournament: a mock battle, fought between individuals or teams of knights with blunted weapons

troubadour: a lyric poet who wrote in the *langue d'oc* of southern France

trouvère: the northern French equivalent of a troubadour

vassal: a person who received a grant of land in return for fealty and service to a lord

Bibliography

IN THEIR OWN WORDS

Bryant, Nigel (trans.) *The History of William Marshal.* Woodbridge: Boydell Press, 2016.

De Charny, Geoffroi. *A Knight's Own Book of Chivalry.* Translated by Elspeth Kennedy. Philadelphia: University of Pennsylvania Press, 2005.

De Pizan, Christine. *The Book of Deeds of Arms and of Chivalry.* Translated by Sumner Willard. University Park, Pa.: Pennsylvania State University Press, 1999.

De Troyes, Chrétien. *Arthurian Romances.* Translated by William W. Kibler. London: Penguin, 1991.

Llull, Ramon. *The Book of the Order of Chivalry.* Translated by Noel Fallows. Woodbridge: Boydell Press, 2013.

Malory, Thomas. *Le Morte d'Arthur.* Translated by Janet Cowen. 2 vols. London: Penguin, 1970.

Matarasso, Pauline M. (trans.) *The Quest of the Holy Grail.* London: Penguin, 1969.

Monmouth, Geoffrey of. *The History of the Kings of Britain.* Translated by Lewis Thorpe. London: Penguin, 1966.

Taylor, Craig and Jane H.M. Taylor (trans.) *The Chivalric Biography of Boucicaut, Jean II Le Meingre.* Woodbridge: Boydell Press, 2016.

Von Eschenbach, Wolfram. *Parzifal.* Translated by A.T. Hatto. London: Penguin, 1980.

Von Liechtenstein, Ulrich. *The Service of Ladies.* Translated by J.W. Thomas. 2nd ed. Woodbridge: Boydell Press, 2004.

MODERN STUDIES

Bachrach, Bernard S. and David S. Bachrach. *Warfare in Medieval Europe, c. 400–c. 1450.* London: Routledge, 2017.

Barber, Richard. *The Knight and Chivalry.* Rev. ed. Woodbridge: Boydell, 1995.

Barber, Richard and Juliet Barker. *Tournaments: Jousts, Chivalry and Pageants in the Middle Ages.* New York: Weidenfeld and Nicolson, 1989.

Bradbury, Jim. *The Routledge Companion to Medieval Warfare.* London: Routledge, 2006.

Crouch, David. *Tournament.* London: Hambledon, 2005.

Crouch, David. *William Marshal.* 3rd ed. London: Routledge, 2016.

DeVries, Kelly. *Infantry Warfare in the Early Fourteenth Century: Discipline, Tactics, and Technology.* Woodbridge: Boydell Press, 1996.

DeVries, Kelly and Robert D. Smith. *Medieval Weapons: An Illustrated History of their Impact.* Santa Barbara: ABC-Clio, 2007.

Harari, Yuval. *Special Operations in the Age of Chivalry, 1100–1500.* Woodbridge: Boydell Press, 2007.

Hyland, Ann. *The Medieval Warhorse: From Byzantium to the Crusades.* London: Grange Books, 1994.

Kaeuper, Richard W. *Holy Warriors: The Religious Ideology of Chivalry.* Philadelphia: University of Pennsylvania Press, 2009.

Kaeuper, Richard W. *Medieval Chivalry.* Cambridge: Cambridge University Press, 2016.

Keen, Maurice. *Chivalry.* New Haven: Yale University Press, 1984.

Keen, Maurice, ed. *Medieval Warfare: A History.* Oxford: Oxford University Press, 1999.

Mondschein, Ken. *The Knightly Art of Battle.* Los Angeles: Getty Publications, 2011.

Morton, Nicholas. *The Medieval Military Orders, 1120–1314.* Harlow: Pearson, 2013.

Nicholson, Helen J. *Medieval Warfare.* New York: Palgrave Macmillan, 2004.

Prestwich, Michael. *Knight: The Medieval Warrior's (Unofficial) Manual.* London: Thames & Hudson, 2010.

Riley-Smith, Jonathan. *The First Crusade and the Idea of Crusading.* 2nd ed. Philadelphia: University of Pennsylvania Press, 2009.

Taylor, Craig. *Chivalry and the Ideals of Knighthood in France during the Hundred Years War.* New York: Cambridge University Press, 2013.

Vernier, Richard. *The Flower of Chivalry: Bertrand du Guesclin and the Hundred Years War.* Woodbridge: Boydell, 2003.

Wright, Nicholas. *Knights and Peasants: The Hundred Years War in the French Countryside.* Woodbridge: Boydell Press, 1998.

Index

Picture Credits

AKG Images: 70 (Collection Joinville)

Alamy: 10 (World History Archive), 13 (Ivy Close Images), 15 (Bildagentur), 18/19 (National Geographic Creative/Tom Lovell), 22 (Ivy Close Images), 27 (ART Collection), 31 (Classic Stock), 33 (Hirarchivum Press), 38 left (The Picture Art Collection), 41 (Universal Images Group/PHAS), 42/43 (Josse Christophel), 46 (Art Collection 2), 48 (The Picture Art Collection), 53 (GL Archive), 54 (Peter Horree), 55 (The Picture Art Collection), 56/57 (Everett Collection), 60 (19th era), 62 (Angelo Hornak), 63 (2d Alan King), 64 (The Picture Art Collection), 66 (Hirarchivum Press), 69 top (Stephen Dorey-Bygone Images), 71 & 72 (Classic Image), 74 bottom (The Picture Art Collection), 75 (Historical Images Archive), 76/77 (Heritage Image Partnerships/Guildhall Art Gallery), 78 (World History Archive), 81 (Josse Christophel), 82 (Timewatch Images), 83 (Falkenstein Heinz-Dieter), 84 (Stock Montage, inc), 87 (Prisma Archivo), 88 (Classic Image), 92 (Glasshouse Images/JT Vintage), 93 (The Projected Art Archive), 94 (Glasshouse Images/JT Vintage), 102 (De Luan), 104 (Ivy Close Images), 106 (Steppenwolf), 107 (Batareykin), 112 (Collection Christophel), 113 (Artokoloro Quint Lox), 115 (Loop Images/Andrew Wilson), 116 (Ross Marks Photography), 120 & 122 (Lanmas), 123 & 125 (Classic Image), 128 &132 (The Picture Art Collection), 133 (Falkensteinphoto), 134 (The Picture Art Collection), 135 (Josse Christobel), 137 (Historical Images Archive), 138 (The History Collection), 139 (The Picture Art Collection), 145 (Historimages Collection/Yolanda Perera Sanchez), 146/147 (De Rocker), 148 (Nigel Reed QEDimages), 149 & 150/151(North Wind Picture Archives), 157 (De Luan), 161 (Walker Art Library), 163 (Picture Art Collection), 168/169 (Josse Christophel), 170 (Blickwinkel/Neukirchen), 171 (Art Collection 2), 172 (Ivy Close Images), 173 (Historical Images Archive), 177 (Panther Media), 178 (Bildagentur-online), 182 top (Pictures Now/Rhoda Schwartz), 183 bottom (CTK/Sojka Libor), 187 (Photo 12/Archives Snark), 191 (World History Archive), 192/193 (Pictorial Press), 196 (North Wind Picture Archive), 197 (Historical Images Archive), 199 (19th Era), 200 (Historical Images Archive), 201 (PBL Collection), 202 (Pictorial Press), 204 (Historical Image Partnerships/Print Collector), 205 (SOTK2011), 209 (ART Collection), 211 (World History Archive), 212 (Art Collection 2), 213 (Active Museum), 214 (Historical Images Archive), 215 (G L Archive), 216 (Print Collector), 217 (World History Archive)

Alamy/Chronicle: 8, 29, 39, 47, 65, 67, 80, 136 both, 152, 167, 182, 190, 203, 210

Alamy/Florilegius: 69 bottom, 74 top, 90, 97, 99, 124, 155, 166 both, 181

Alamy/Granger Collection: 9, 35, 36/37, 38 right, 40, 45, 116/117, 129, 153, 156, 208

Alamy/Heritage Image Partnerships/Fine Art Archive: 20/21, 42, 50/51, 58, 118/119, 126/127, 159, 160, 174, 179, 180

Alamy/Interfoto: 14, 16 top, 44, 73, 100 bottom, 103, 105 both, 110 both, 164, 184

Alamy/Science History Images/Photo Researchers: 11, 34, 86, 130/131, 158, 176

Amber Books: 12 both, 114, 144

Bridgeman Images: 68 (British Library), 206/207 (Palacio del Senado, Madrid)

Depositphotos: 24/25 (Jorisvo), 98 (Nejron), 101 (Friday), 111 (Bloodua), 140 (Georgios), 195 (Catncia-01)

Dreamstime: 7 (Mariusz Prusaczyk), 21 (Carlos Soler Martinez), 164/165 (Didewide), 194 (John Holmes)

Getty Images: 59 (Time Life Picture Collection), 91 (Hulton), 96 (Roger Viollet), 175 (Ullstein Bild), 186 (Universal Images Group/Christophel Fine Art), 188 (Gamma-Rapho/Jean-Erick Pasquier), 198 (Hulton)

Getty Images/De Agostini: 6, 17 (C. Balossini), 26, 28, 30, 32 (Dagli Orti), 108/109, 141 (G. Nimatallah), 142/143 (Dagli Orti), 154

Giogo/Wikipedia: 100 top (CC by SA 4.0)